T0300110

ROUTLEDGE LIBRARY EDITIONS: INFLATION

Volume 2

WAGE RESTRAINT AND THE CONTROL OF INFLATION

WAGE RESTRAINT AND THE CONTROL OF INFLATION

An International Survey

Edited by
BETH BILSON

Routledge
Taylor & Francis Group

LONDON AND NEW YORK

First published in 1987 by Croom Helm/St. Martin's Press, Inc.

This edition first published in 2016
by Routledge
2 Park Square, Milton Park, Abingdon, Oxon OX14 4RN

and by Routledge
711 Third Avenue, New York, NY 10017

Routledge is an imprint of the Taylor & Francis Group, an informa business

© 1987 R. E. Bilson

British Library Cataloguing in Publication Data
A catalogue record for this book is available from the British Library

ISBN: 978-1-138-65251-4 (Set)
ISBN: 978-1-315-62042-8 (Set) (ebk)
ISBN: 978-1-138-65252-1 (Volume 2) (hbk)
ISBN: 978-1-315-62418-1 (Volume 2) (ebk)

Publisher's Note
The publisher has gone to great lengths to ensure the quality of this reprint but points out that some imperfections in the original copies may be apparent.

Disclaimer
The publisher has made every effort to trace copyright holders and would welcome correspondence from those they have been unable to trace.

WAGE RESTRAINT AND THE CONTROL OF INFLATION

An International Survey

Edited by Beth Bilson

Scholarly & Reference Division,
St. Martin's Press, Inc., 175 Fifth Avenue, New York, NY 10010
First published in the United States of America in 1987
Printed in Great Britain

Library of Congress Cataloging-in-Publication Data

Wage restraint and the control of inflation.

  Bibliography: p.
  Includes index.
  1. Unemployment — United States — Effect of
inflation on. 2. Unemployment — Australia —
Effect of inflation on. 3. Unemployment —
Canada — Effect of inflation on. 4. Unemployment —
Germany (West) — Effect of inflation on.
I. Bilson, Beth.
HD5724.W24 1987   339.5   86-22575
ISBN 0-312-00374-9

CONTENTS

ACKNOWLEDGMENTS

The marshalling of contributions from several sources is always a complicated task, and the editor is grateful for the assistance of a number of people in the preparation of this manuscript. Thanks must go to Bernice Noton, Natalie McLeod and Martha Michelmann, who typed much of the original manuscript, and to the staff of typingPLUS Inc. for their assistance in preparing the final copy.

In addition, the editor is grateful to the President's Fund of the University of Saskatchewan for financial support.

INTRODUCTION

The industrialised nations of the world have had an exciting ride since the end of the Second World War. For most of those countries, the period was until recently one of the great - in the case of Germany and Japan, one might say miraculous - economic prosperity, of nurture of the welfare state, and of optimism about continued economic growth. The people of these nations have enjoyed an unprecedented level of material comfort and economic security, which it appeared they could hope continually to enhance.

In the 1970s, however, doubts were increasingly voiced about the soundness of the foundations on which this amazing structure stood. The shock of the petroleum crisis of 1973 was perhaps the major factor leading to a reorientation of the industrialised world, but there were others - the instability of food prices, the growing insistence of the less industrialised countries on a voice in the setting of international economic policy while their own economic problems placed an increasing strain on that policy, the rise of a very public advocacy directed at environmental issues, to name a few.

One of the problems associated with the economic history of the post-war period has been inflation. Inflation has, of course, a certain symbolic value for politicians and economic decision-makers, because of their swift association of the word with wheelbarrowloads of worthless marks in the 1920s, or with the more recent economic desperation of countries like Argentina. Throughout the last several decades, inflation has been viewed as a serious threat to the goal of economic growth and prosperity, more or less serious at various moments, but always requiring some attention in the

1

course of economic policy-making.

Discussion of any topic with economic implications has been complicated by the differences of outlook between the Keynesian and neoclassical modes of economic thought which have dominated the policies of western nations. For three and a half decades after 1945, the assumptions on which economic policy proceeded by and large, were grounded in a Keynesian or crypto-Keynesian view of the world; though governments might deviate from Keynesian orthodoxy in various ways there was underlying consensus about the efficacy of some sort of demand-management technique and an acceptance of government's role in guiding the economy.

The late 1970s saw the rise (or perhaps resurgence) of interest in neoclassical theory, and the renewal of a commitment to the forces of the market as the preferable fountain-head of economic activity. Governments with a specific commitment to supply-side economic policy were elected in a number of countries, including several of those discussed here, and supply-side ideas influenced policy development and debate elsewhere.

There are certain obstacles to any comparison or even coherent discussion of these two views since they count their successes and describe their objectives in terms sufficiently different that they can hardly be talked about as though they operate on the same plane.

This volume is concerned with wage inflation, and more particularly, with the measures taken by a number of industrialised countries to combat wage inflation. Already, in this description of the book's compass, a problem appears, for the use of terms like 'measures' and 'combat' suggest that we are only concerned here with positive action undertaken with a view to bring wage inflation under control.

In fact, the Keynesian and the supply-side policy-makers approach this problem from different directions, or perhaps define it as a different problem. From the neoclassical point of view, the problem is one of liberating economic forces so that they may moderate wage inflation in their own way, while the Keynesian theorists see the question rather as one of what combination of economic tools should be used to guide the economy in the desired direction.

This is - it goes without saying - a simplistic version of these economic theories, and describes in terms of polarity what is really a much more complex and differentiated continuum of economic thought. It is put in these terms to indicate the range of economic outlook travelled by governments in the post-war period.

In implementing the tenets of variants of these economic theories, governments have from time to time adopted or invented what might be called incomes policies; though incomes policies themselves vary widely in sophistication in objectives and in rigour, the term may be roughly defined to include those policies where the objective is to moderate wage inflation in some organised way. More recently, the use of incomes policies has been in some cases replaced by what could be described as anti-policy to suggest the neoclassical determination to eschew the utilisation of government instruments to pursue economic improvement.

The essays in this volume deal with both incomes policy and anti-policy; they represent an attempt both to describe what approaches have been taken at various points by the governments of selected countries, and also to indicate what the effects of those policy choices have been.

None of the contributors to this book make their living as economists and economists will perhaps be critical of the temerity shown by us in embarking on a discussion of economic policy. Yet, in our view, economic policy is too important to be left entirely to those trained to be economists. Economists themselves are generally not shy about mounting a critique of politics, educational policy, or other social phenomena on the grounds that they have economic implications. Equally, it is arguably legitimate to examine economic policies with special attention to the effects they have on a society and on the citizens within that society. What we have tried to do here is to sketch some of the implications which these policies have in the non-economic sphere.

The survey format brings with it certain frustrations both for the writers and the readers, for it is inevitable that generalisations must be made, outlines must be blurred rather than sharp, important shadings must be omitted. The advantage of this form in dealing with this particular subject is that it can convey, as perhaps nothing else could, the astonishing variety of ways in which these countries have characterised and confronted the wage inflation problem.

To begin with, of course, the five countries whose experience is described here represent a range of political, constitutional and social systems which must be understood to at least a minimal degree before specific policy choices can be evaluated. Several features of the national life of these countries are of particular importance in a discussion of their respective approaches to inflation: the constitutional arrangements which may affect economic policy; the political system, particularly as it touches the roles of labour and of business in the society and - a more indefinable characteristic - the stand of the society to questions of social justice and economic redistribution.

The term 'constitutional' is somewhat ambiguous when applied to the countries discussed in these pages. In Canada, for example, the constitutional question has traditionally been one of the proper allocation of legislative jurisdiction to national or provincial governments. This has also been an issue in Australia. This continuing tension over the appropriate jurisdiction for economic policy-making reflects differing-regional interests and political outlooks; the stance of the Canadian province of Quebec, for example, is informed in part by French-Canadian nationalism, while the governments of several other provinces have been influenced by their dependence on natural resources.

More recently in Canada however, another type of constitutional issue has surfaced, concerning the impact of an enumeration of protected rights and freedoms on the making of economic policy and the status of economic actors such as trade unions. In West Germany, where constitutionally-entrenched protection extends specifically to economic activity, the same issue arises as to the permissible scope of economic measures which may affect such protected activity. Oddly enough this issue has not been raised in quite this way in the United States, where there has also been entrenchment of rights and freedoms over a long period of time.

A more pertinent constitutional issue in the United States relates to the disposition of influence between the branches of the governmental system; as we shall see, much of American policy directed to wage inflation has depended on the influence of the Presidency. This aspect of the constitutional inquiry perhaps surfaces in its commonest form in the assertion, common to all these countries, of judicial authority to interpret economic legislation, to adjudicate the rights of various economic actors and to limit the exercise of executive or legislative power. Political developments in any country are clearly relevant to the course taken by economic policy, as are the shifting political relationships of constituent groups in any society. The relationship which has most immediate influence on policies concerning wages is that between any government and the labour and business constituencies.

The business sector of any industrialised society generally has access to a number of instruments of political influence, through lobbying, through political contributions, through utilisation of the government industrial policy. The representation of labour and the role of trade unions is far more uneasy, owing partly to the hostility of these states to early trade union activity. The importance of labour acquiescence in economic policy is now widely acknowledged nonetheless, and the support of workers for measures to control wage inflation has on occasion been actively sought and, indeed, been made a cornerstone of restraint policy.

The form this may take depends greatly on the nature of labour's participation in the political life of its society. In European countries including Great Britain, labour typically speaks in the political forum through political organisations which purportedly embody the aspirations and interests of workers. This allows labour to exercise a degree of direct political clout and renders possible the implementation of the kind of policy often referred to as a 'social contract,' in which labour may co-operate in forwarding government economic policies in return for governments's acceptance of certain labour objectives.

Clearly, the social contract type of policy, which has appeared in various guises, is more likely to be put into effect when a government representing labour, or at least sympathetic to it, is in power. Under those circumstances both labour and 'its' government are more aware of the mutual gains which may be made, and there is a greater degreee of the trust necessary to reach agreement on the policy. Thus, in Great Britain, for example, leaving aside the Social Contract of the mid-1970s, there were several other periods when trade unions made clear their expectations of a Labour government and agreed to lend their support to restraint policy, in return.

For non-labour governments as well, the benefits of winning labour support are obvious. The

most common way of trying to marshall this support
has been through the creation of tri-partite bodies
to serve as a focus for the discussion of economic
policy. Though these bodies have on occasion echoed
with acrimony, and with harsh denunciations of
government policy, in Europe, at least, these
syndicalist mechanisms have generally survived as a
vital force.

In North America, it is perhaps fair to say
that neither direct political action by labour nor
tri-partism have really been influential factors,
though both have surfaced in Canada and the United
States. The strength of the two-party system in
American politics has pretty well foreclosed the
possibility of a 'labour' party in the United States
though the union movement has traditional ties - and
even a degree of influence - with the Democratic
party. In Canada, there is a social democratic
party which ostensibly represents labour, but which
exerts limited influence on the national political
scene.

Various attempts have been made at tri-partite
discussion in both countries, but, perhaps because
of their degree of political disenfranchisement, the
labour movement has been wary of such arrangements.
Thus, in Canada, a flurry of enthusiasm for tri-
partism among officials of the Canadian Labour
Congress was quelled in 1978 when it became evident
that constituent unions were cool to the idea. In
any event, the decentralised nature of North
American collective bargaining and trade union
organisation raised difficult issues regarding
representation and the co-ordination of activity on
a national scale. It has been argued, as well, that
the weakness of class identification, in the
European sense, has made it difficult to sustain
tri-partite discussion in North America.

It is obvious that a survey of this sort can
really do no more than hint at the stand which any
society may take at any given point to issues of
redistribution or social justice. There are, of
course, certain clues which may be gathered from the
nature of policies which are adopted. One may
conclude - from the inclusion of a low-pay exception
to wage limits or from the orientation of a given
policy towards the market - certain things about the
commitment of a nation to the adjustment of income
levels or shares in national wealth, but these are
rarely made explicit, and there is not room to
explore them fully within these pages.

The kinds of national characteristics which

have been sketched here - and numerous other threads, from Domesday Book and Martin Luther to Botany Bay, the Canadian Pacific Railway and the New Deal, which cannot even be alluded to here - form the background against which the struggle to defeat wage inflation has taken place. Though the experience of these countries has varied a great deal, there are certain features which have recurred from time to time and place to place, and the measures attempted have exhibited some characteristics common enough to suggest a theme, if not a pattern.

At some point or another, it would appear that almost every imaginable type of policy which might have an effect on wage inflation has been attempted - though no doubt, there are some which have yet to be imagined. There have been positive and passive policies, policies which depended on the power of persuasion and policies backed up by statutory sanctions, measures which articulated very specific objectives and those which merely pointed a general direction.

Within the range of policies which define themselves as incomes policies, as opposed to those which reject that tag, there have been many kinds of administrative mechanism devised to advance the aim of restraint of wage inflation. At times these have been quite elaborate; one thinks of the Canadian Anti-Inflation Board with its staff of a thousand. At other times there has been no purpose-built structure, and monitoring has been conducted by an ordinary government department or official. In some cases, mechanisms devised for other purposes have assumed an important role in wage restraint. This would include the courts, in some sense, but perhaps the clearest example is the Australian Conciliation and Arbitration Commission, which has proved so amenable to use as part of incomes policy.

Much of the administrative tone of any policy is likely to be set by the choice of whether to attempt to monitor all wage settlements or to focus on settlements which are regarded as sufficiently significant as to set the pattern for other agreements. The notion of 'key settlements' has figured large from time to time in most of the countries here surveyed; it has been addressed particularly explicitly at some periods in the United States, and elaborated by American economic theorists.

In a way, the idea of pattern-setting or key

settlements has been implicit in much of the
discussion and the decision-making concerning how
the public sector wages are to be dealt with. The
flowering of public sector employment in the post-
war Keynesian state, along with the recognition that
public sector wages are not determined and do not
move in the same way as those in the private sector,
have inevitably caused the public sector to be
accorded a different kind of attention in any
incomes policy. One common manifestation of this
has been the kind of policy in which the government
attempts to set a good example for the rest of
society by imposing limits on the wage increase of
its own employees. This kind of policy has obvious
political attractions, though there is very little
evidence that private sector wages do follow the
example set in the public sector.

The recent period of neoclassical influence has
produced its own version of this policy. Supply-
side policy-makers would not describe it as an
incomes policy, in that they eschew all policies
which could divert the forces of the market. Nonetheless, it is clear that one of their major
objectives is to cut back the level of government
spending, and thus reduce the dependence of the
economy on the public sector; attempts to achieve
this aim can have an effect on the wages of public
sector employees not unlike that of a formal incomes
policy, as unions representing public employees
vociferously point out. Insofar as governments must
make conscious decisions about the wage levels which
they will accord to their employees, there will
inevitably be some sort of 'incomes policy' in
effect, even for a government which is in other
sectors opposed to such policies.

Besides the choice as to whether a policy
should be comprehensive or merely cover key settlements, and whether it should depend on the moral
force of the public sector example or extend to
private sector settlements as well, the choice must
also be made when an incomes policy is decided upon,
to count on voluntary public compliance with the
limits placed by the scheme or to provide formal
sanctions in the event of delinquency. The search
for an appropriate balance between voluntarism and
coercion is a feature in the construction of much
public policy; it is arguable that the legislative
and administrative hallmark of a democratic society
is the striving after consensus which can make a
minimum of coercion necessary.

Both voluntary and mandatory control programmes

have been tested at various times in the post-war history of the countries discussed in this volume, and both have had some success at achieving their objectives. Sheer moral suasion has on occasion, produced widespread self-restraint, as in Britain in the time of the austere Sir Stafford Cripps. At the other end of the spectrum there have been elaborate systems of formal sanctions, such as the fines and rollbacks available to the Canadian Anti-Inflation Administrator. Social contract policies on the lines of that in Australia recently or Britain in the mid 1970s are perhaps examples of what might be called 'formal self-discipline,' indicating an acknowledgment by the labour movement that it was necessary for them to assume responsibility for the direction of compensation trends.

It is again difficult to categorize 1980s economic policy regarding wages according to the principles mentioned earlier. To those policy-makers persuaded by supply-side arguments, voluntarism is more or less irrelevant, as it has Keynesian overtones of human control over economic forces. There can, as well, be little doubt that the depressing effect on wages of the high levels of unemployment, accepted with such stoicism by those same policy-makers, cannot be described as resting on voluntarism in the usual sense.

The choice of mandatory or voluntary controls depends in part on an assessment of likely public support for a regime of restraint, and that public temper is critical to the success of any incomes policy.

It is submitted that the consideration which most affects the sentiment of the public towards an incomes policy - and this, I suggest, includes the non-policies of the neoclassically-oriented decision-makers - is the public perception of that policy's fairness. This demand for fairness encompasses several things.

It takes in, first of all, the question of whether the form of any incomes policy satisfies whatever the public sees as the reasonable requirements of redistributive justice. It can certainly be argued that the interests of the low-paid (and the unemployed) are fairly cheerfully consigned to the flames when any period of restraint is announced, and that they suffer disproportionately from the pressure of limits on wages. Nonetheless, it is fairly common that formal incomes policies make some attempt to mitigate the harm to the low-paid by relaxing the limits in their case.

Introduction

Perhaps a more critical factor in public apprehension of the fairness of a policy concerning wages is whether that policy addresses itself to the moderation of prices and profits as well. Some of the policies which will be examined later have included a full range of controls to tackle the price question; this does not, of course, always prevent continuing criticism from the labour movement and others that the price control aspect of the programme is mere window-dressing, and that government policy-makers are at heart committed to a wage-push theory of inflation. This view has on occasion been fuelled by sophisticated explanations to the effect that pricing decisions are of a more complex nature than wage settlements and thus cannot effectively be controlled by a government policy.

As we shall see, it may be difficult to arrive at any firm conclusion as to whether the price control mechanisms which have been adopted have been effective in meeting their goals; whatever evidence may be advanced one way or the other, the sense of wage-earners that it is they who are being asked to make disproportionate sacrifices in the struggle against inflation may have a powerful influence over public support for a restraint programme.

In an assessment of wage restraint as such, a major criterion of fairness in public eyes which might be suggested is uniformity. As long as a wage restraint policy seems to be affecting all segments of society in the same way, it appears to have a better chance of maintaining public support. This poses something of a problem for those in charge of constructing the instruments of wage restraint, for the necessity to maintain uniformity puts them on the horns of a dilemma over whether the programme should hinge on the setting of norms (or guidelines, guideposts or guiding lights) and, if so, how those standards should be calculated.

If a norm or fixed limit of some kind is adopted, it has the virtue of providing an instant impression of justice, of the consistent application of one standard to all persons. The use of norms has some drawbacks, however. One of these is that the validity of the norm itself may come into question, either because there is open dispute about the way it has been calculated, or because it proves as time goes on to bear no relation to the course taken by inflation. In either event, there appears to be a tendency for public support to weaken and consensus to disappear as the anomalies which inhered in the wage pattern at the outset become more exaggerated and the guidelines become increasingly oppressive in the eyes of those who enjoy a disadvantaged position because of this.

For this reason, a policy in which norms or guidelines are not set out has attracted policymakers. Such a policy allows wage settlements to be addressed in their own context, and provides sufficient flexibility for anomalies to be considered; it has been argued that only by such a relativistic approach is there hope for the long-term adjustment of wage patterns. Of course, this type of policy is vulnerable to public restiveness for a different reason than those programmes with fixed norms: such decisions must always in some respects be open to charges of arbitrariness and ad-hocism, for the criteria on which these judgments depend are bound to be elusive and difficult to articulate. The policy which was most ambitious in this respect, in the 1960s in Great Britain, succumbed eventually to the pressure for fixed norms, after which the general level of support for the programme declined rapidly.

Closely tied to the dilemma posed by the disadvantages both of norms and their absence is the essential issue of whether any given policy has as its objective effective response to an immediate economic problem, real or perceived, or whether its aims are more ambitious and extend to long-term control over wage patterns. If there is any conclusion which can be drawn from the tangled web which is about to be placed before you, it is that no government has yet succeeded in discovering a mechanism by which wage inflation can be stabilised over the longer term. Judgment should perhaps be reserved on this point with respect to those supply-side policies which have recently been followed, though one wonders whether the dampening effect they have apparently had on inflation can be sustained in a period of vigorous economic recovery.

There are a number of factors contributing to the so-far unsolved riddle of instability in wage control policy. One factor is, of course, the difficulty of economic prediction in any circumstances, the problems of taking into account the unpredictable and projecting for the unforeseeable, which confounds even the most thoughtful economic policy.

The majority of policies chosen in most of these countries, thus far, have been exercises in crisis management, attempts to deal with immediate economic problems. Commitment to longer-term

policies, which may be effective only over a genera-
tion, is a lot to ask of the 'social partners' in
any democratic country. Their own objectives and
ambitions and their own means of assessment are
measured in the life of year-end balance sheets,
collective agreements and periods between elections;
anything which can only defer results or promise
consequences in the future is difficult for the
parties to defend. Yet the crisis response type of
policy seems to carry within it possible seeds of
further crisis and it is unlikely to confront any of
the structural imbalances or fundamental forces of
the wage system.

The surprising thing is perhaps that governments make ever-renewed attempts at controlling wage
inflation, and that the populations of these
countries seem amenable to such new attempts, in
some cases with optimism, in some with resignation.
The story of incomes policies in the industrialised
world is as much one of a psychological as an
economic phenomenon. And if the questions raised by
such a judgment were ever to be answered, we would
stand at the threshold of a different age indeed.

Chapter One

UNITED STATES: CONTROL IN THE FREE MARKET

John Lawler

INTRODUCTION

Despite an ideological aversion in the United States
to the direct setting of wages and prices by
government, such programmes, in various forms and
degrees of intensity, have appeared periodically
from the time of the American Revolution. However,
the implementation of guidelines or controls has
always been viewed as a short-term expedient for
containing particular bouts of inflation. Moreover,
American policy makers have typically avoided use of
the expression 'incomes policy,' symbolizing, among
other things, the view that government ought to
avoid a permanent role in the setting of wages and
prices. Despite this position, general wage-price
guidelines, controls, or freezes have been in effect
during roughly one-third of the past 50 years.
Formal wage-price restraint programmes over the
period include:

1. 1942-1946: World War II; wage-price
   controls (Roosevelt-Truman administra-
   tions);
2. 1951-1953: Korean War; wage-price controls
   (Truman administration);
3. 1962-1966: Voluntary wage-price guidelines
   (Kennedy-Johnson administration);
4. 1971-1973: Wage-price controls (Nixon
   administration);
5. 1978-1980: Voluntary wage-price guidelines
   (Carter administration).

Although this chapter focuses on formal and
economy-wide wage policies, the reader should keep
in mind that the federal government in the United
States intervenes into the wage and price setting

13

process in a variety of other ways. Prices in certain industries – public utilities, for example – are regulated by either state or federal agencies. Absent formal controls or guidelines, the President or another high-ranking administration official may intercede when major wage settlements or pricing decisions are seen to be inflationary. Of course, wage and price policies are not always directed at limiting inflation; minimum wage and 'fair trade' laws, first enacted during the Depression, specify wage and price floors, though most fair trade laws have now been repealed.

This chapter will treat the subject of wage and price restraint programs in the United States in three parts. First, the theoretical arguments regarding the usefulness – or dangers – of incomes policies, as formulated in relation to the American economy, will be considered. The second section of the chapter will trace the evolution of American policy from the Second World War through the Reagan administration, focusing on particular programmes and the forces shaping those programmes. Finally, incomes policies in the United States will be evaluated in terms of past successes and failures and future usefulness.

THEORY AND POLICY

An understanding of American wage and price policies and assessments of these policies requires that we review alternative theoretical perspectives on inflation and its relationship to aggregate economic activity. Differing perspectives are considered here, with emphasis on policy implications.

The Phillips Curve and Institutional Analysis: Early Formulations

The work of A.W. Phillips[1] and Richard Lipsey[2] on the apparent relationship between the unemployment rate and nominal wage inflation in Great Britain had a profound effect on American thought. The 'discovery' of the Phillips relation coincided with the emergence and establishment of Keynesian thought as the dominant force in the formation of American economic policy. Although the Phillips relationship was not completely consistent with Keynesian theory in its original form (which did not posit an inflation/unemployment trade-off), it nonetheless implied that nominal wages and prices

14

had relatively permanent effects on the real level
of economic activity. Thus, 'full employment' was
not seen to be achieved at some determinant,
equilibrium level of employment (or unemployment);
rather, policy-makers could choose from a menu of
unemployment and inflation rates, their choices
depending upon the perceived social costs and
benefit of increasing prices versus those of
diminished output and employment.

The Phillips curve gained prominence in America
as the result of a paper by Paul Samuelson and
Robert Solow.[3] There followed a series of
empirical studies designed to assess the validity of
the Phillips relationship in the American economy,
the most notable being Perry's estimation of a
multi-equation model depicting the interrelation-
ships among wages, prices, and profits.[4] American
scholars did not buy fully the argument of a long-
term, relatively fixed relationship between wage
inflation and unemployment, as presented by Phillips. This reluctance was attributable, in large
part, to the debate over 'cost-push' and 'demand-
pull' theories of inflation. The assumption of a
stable Phillips curve was clearly consistent with
the demand-pull school of thought, which saw inflationary pressures as dependent on change in the
demand for labour. Cost-push pressures, on the
other hand, were thought to arise from institutional
forces, especially collective bargaining, union
power, and administered prices under imperfect
competition. Changes in market structure, inter-
market mobility, and union power and wage policies
could be expected to impact on wage inflation
exogenously, leading to structural changes in the
Phillips curve. Given the evident power of American
unions in the early 1960s, it is not surprising that
the institutionalist argument carried considerable
weight.

In addition to market structure and union power
considerations, institutionalists maintained that
wage-setting practices in both union and non-union
settings could create or accentuate inflationary
pressures. A central theme of institutionalist
analysis was the notion of wage spillover and pattern bargaining. Dunlop, for example, proposed the
existence of 'wage contours' - groupings of firms
and industries in which general wage levels moved in
relative unison.[5] Wages were seen to be determined initially in the 'key' firms, bargaining
units, or industries within a particular cluster,
with market conditions affecting the relevant wage-

setting unit laying an important role in the process. The unemployment rate was hypothesised to have a transitory effect on the relative distribution of union-management bargaining power, with union power enhanced in periods of low unemployment. In addition, the cost of living, an employer's ability to pay, and exogenous sources of union power such as the degree of unionisation or employer product market concentration, were also often hypothesised as determinants of wage settlements in key units. Wages determined in key units were hypothesised to set the pattern for non-key units within the cluster. Thus, market conditions in non-key units were seen to play a secondary role, at best, in the determination of wages in those units. In other words, the Phillips relationship, albeit modified, held for key, but not non-key, units. Key units were thought to be in those heavily unionised sectors of the economy in which employers enjoyed considerable product market power, while non-key units were seen to be in weakly organised or non-union sectors in which firms had little product market power. Empirical support for the spillover hypothesis came in the form of intensive case studies of wage-setting practices[6] and, later, multivariate statistical analyses.[7]

An idealised version of the institutionalist wage-setting process, within a particular wage contour, would be of the following form:

(1.1) $w(k) = a(0) + [a(1)][1/Un(k)] + [a(2)][p] + [a(3)][R(k)] + [a(4)][(X(k)]$

(1.2) $w(nk) = b(0) = [b(1)][w(k)] + [b(2)]X(nk)]$

where: $w(k)$, $w(nk)$ = wage change in key, non-key units; $Un(k)$ = unemployment rate affecting key units; p = change in consumer prices; $R(k)$ = profit rate of firms in key units; $X(k)$, $X(nk)$ = composite of other exogenous influences affecting key, non-key units.

In its strong form, the spillover argument posits that $b(1)$ approaches unity; consequently, wage changes in key groups are nearly completely transmitted to non-key groups. Wage increases translate into price changes via some cost adjustment process:

(2) $p = w - q$

where: w = economy-wide, average change in wages; q

16

= economy-wide average change in productivity.

The wage and price adjustment processes depicted in these equations suggest that both cost-push and demand-pull forces may either concurrently or separately lead to inflation. Demand-pull forces, however, were viewed as working through transitory shifts in the distribution of bargaining power between union and management rather than through market adjustments to excess labour supply or demand. Despite the demand-side influences included in the model, cost-push pressures were clearly seen as dominant in the institutionalist analysis. Cost-push pressures could initiate an inflationary epoch, as could demand-pull pressures; moreover, cost-push pressures could accentuate or perpetuate inflationary epochs long after excess demand had diminished. In particular, the institutionalist perspective suggested the possibility of a wage-price spiral that could not be explained in terms of neoclassical market processes. The intensity and destabilising potential of the wage-price spiral would depend upon the elasticity of wage inflation with respect to price inflation, as with, for example, $a(2)$ in Equation (1.1). Thus, stabilisation policies that depended exclusively on the manipulation of conventional monetary and fiscal variables were apt to be ineffective unless supplemented by policies addressing the institutional sources of inflation. Consider the following scenarios that might arise in this system:

1. Transitory inflation (demand-induced): Excess demand in key units increases key wage inflation, leading to increased non-key wage inflation. Price inflation increases by the average change in wage inflation, minus any offsetting productivity gains. Higher wages in key sectors lead to increased unemployment in key sectors, resulting in lower key wage inflation. Assuming $a(2)<1.0$, then inflation and unemployment return, <u>ceteris paribus</u>, reasonably quickly to pre-disturbance levels.

2. Transitory inflation (cost-induced): An increase in union power resulting from shifts in exogenous variables affecting key unit settlements (i.e., $X(k)$) leads to increased key wage inflation, which is

17

transmitted to non-key units. Price inflation increases by the average change in wage inflation, minus any offsetting productivity gains. Higher wages in key sectors lead to increased unemployment in key sectors, resulting in lower key wage inflation. Assuming $a(2)<1.0$, then inflation returns, _ceteris paribus_, reasonably quickly to pre-disturbance levels. However, unemployment is likely to remain higher than pre-disturbance levels.

3. Protracted/accelerating inflation: Depending upon the values of the coefficient of the model, either demand- or cost-induced inflation may lead to a protracted bout of possibly accelerating inflation - the wage-price spiral in its classic and most pernicious form. In order for this to occur, price elasticity in the key sector equation, i.e., $a(2)$, must approach a value of 1.0 and/or the unemployment/wage change relationship must be relatively weak in key unit settlements. In addition, price elasticity terms may appear in the non-key unit functions, as would be the case, for example, with cost-of-living indexed contracts. Thus, wage increases would be reinforced through price increases. Efforts by employers in relatively noncompetitive, key unit industries, endeavouring to raise profit margins by increasing prices, could also initiate an inflationary epoch - 'profit-push' inflation. The unemployment presumably created by escalating wages and prices would exert a counter-balancing influence; however, since non-key sectors are not influenced (or only weakly influenced) by market conditions, and since key unit contracts may only be renegotiated every two or three years, demand-side pressures could only slow inflation in the very long term. Consequently, once initiated, an inflationary epoch would tend to be protracted. The greater the value of the price elasticity terms, the greater would be the equilibrium level of inflation. If the elasticity terms equalled or exceeded 1.0 in both the wage and price adjustment functions, then the system could become unstable, with continually accelerating

rates of inflation.

The processes depicted in Scenarios 1 and 2, especially the former, are fairly consistent with the conventional Phillips curve framework. Assuming reasonably rapid key unit adjustments to changes in the unemployment rate, then fiscal and monetary tools would be appropriate to stabilise inflation and unemployment. Yet, by the early 1960s, multi-year labour contracts were quite common in the United States,[8] thus dampening the unemployment/ wage change relationship. There had also been considerable experimentation with price inflation indexation in labour contracts, especially during the Korean War. Even in the absence of explicit cost-of-living adjustment (COLA) clauses, many thought past experiences with inflation or 'catch-up' pressures resulting from under-anticipated inflation were of considerable significance in shaping contract clauses. Hence, the conditions necessary to create Scenario 3 inflation were believed prevalent by many institutionalist writers.

Although some authors suggested the need to consider policies designed to decentralise bargaining in certain key sectors, thus decreasing spillover pressures and pattern bargaining, most institutionalists were also committed to free collective bargaining and relatively strong unions. Consequently, emphasis was placed on selective wage and price restraint in key sectors. By identifying noninflationary wage and price adjustment formulae, it was argued that inflationary pressures created by institutional practices could be reduced or eliminated. Rather than arguing for a system of explicit wage and price controls, 'guidelines' were advocated, with government officials, and occasionally the President, endeavouring to persuade labour and management representatives in key units to follow these guidelines.

The Neoclassical Challenge and the 'Natural Unemployment Rate'

The late 1960s and early 1970s witnessed, in the United States, increasing inflation coupled with increasing unemployment. Neoclassical economists saw this largely as the consequence of the misguided notions underlying the neo-Keynesian Phillips curve. Despite the lip-service paid to the role of institutional processes, the Phillips curve analysis, they

19

argued, rests largely on the existence of long-term money illusion, which contradicts assumptions of rational economic decision-making. Both Phelps[9] and Friedman[10] developed models which incorporated inflationary expectations into wage and price adjustment functions, demonstrating that a permanent trade-off between unemployment and steady-state inflation could not exist. A series of essays edited by Phelps[11] expanded on this theme, constructing a micro-economic framework for the analysis of aggregate labour market activity.

The basic position of the neoclassical critics of the Phillips curve as well as of institutionalist theories of cost-push inflation, is that the institutional setting within which wage determination takes place is largely window-dressing. Wages are determined through competitive market adjustment processes in which individual employers and employees seek optimal contracts, although some formulations assume a degree of employer monopsony. The labour market is modelled as a system of flows of individuals among various labour force states – employed, unemployed, not in labour force. The unemployment rate is determined by the dynamic equilibrium of competing flows,[12] which stands in contrast to earlier static formulations. In the short run, individuals may have wage expectations based on outdated information. Thus, the perceived real wage may be greater than the true real wage, given current prices, which would lead to reduced unemployment; the converse occurs when inflationary expectations exceed actual inflation. This would generate a short-run Phillips curve relationship.

In the long run, however, expectations are argued to adjust to shifting inflationary conditions. Rational economic actors should, in fairly short order, assimilate new information and adjust wage bargains accordingly. Thus, unlike in the Phillips curve and institutionalist formulations, employers and employees project future rates of inflation and act on such expectations, rather than simply reacting with a significant lag to past inflation. This approach has come to be known as the 'rational expectations' perspective and is closely associated with the so-called 'natural rate' hypothesis.[13] Within the natural rate framework, the issue of key versus non-key unit distinction is irrelevant; indeed, the role of collective bargaining in wage-setting is often simply ignored. Thus, the economy-wide wage adjustment function is written as:

$$(3) \quad w = [c(1)][Un] + [c(7)][w*]$$

where: w = economy-wide, average rate of change of
wages; Un = economy-wide unemployment rate; w* =
expected rate of change in wages. The expected rate
of change in wages should depend on the expected
rate of inflation (p*) and the expected change in
productivity (q*):

$$(4) \quad w* = p* + q*$$

Given perfect foresight with respect to the rate of
price inflation and productivity growth, then, in
the long term, the actual and expected rates of wage
inflation will coincide, i.e., w* = w. Substituting
this into Equation (3) and rearranging terms to
solve for w in terms of Un, we obtain:

$$(5) \quad w = [c(1)][1/Un]/[1-c(2)]$$

Since rational economic actors will completely
incorporate inflationary expectations into wage
bargains, the coefficient of the expectations term
(c(2)) ought to equal 1.00. Under those circumstances, the denominator of the expression on the
right-hand side of Equation (5) is equal to zero and
the Phillips curve reduces to a vertical line. In
other words, there can be no long-term inflation/
unemployment trade-off; there is a single equilibrium unemployment rate (the 'natural unemployment
rate') and efforts to maintain the unemployment rate
below the natural rate by conventional demand management techniques can only result in accelerating
inflation and an apparently worsening inflation/
unemployment trade-off.
    The specific policy implications emerging from
the analysis of contemporary neoclassical economists
are often charteracterised collectively as 'supply-
side' economics; as a consequence of the close
identification of supply-side economics with the
current administration, the approach has also been
dubbed 'Reaganomics.' The expression reflects the
rehabilitation of Say's Law - supply creates its own
demand - implicit in this perspective. It is argued
that the manipulation of the economy through
monetary and especially fiscal policy have distorted
normal market mechanisms, discouraged capital
investment, and thus slowed productivity and
economic growth. Inflation, high interest rates,
extensive government regulation of business, and tax
laws in the tradition of the New Deal are viewed as

primarily responsible. Supply-side economists advocate policies which they argue will increase potential output and lead to the efficient operation of markets, so as to realise such increases in the real level of economic activity.

Needless to say, advocates of the supply-side perspective take a dim view of incomes policies or wage and price controls. These are argued to distort market processes. Even if effective in the short run, there is sure to be a day of reckoning once the controls have been lifted. The conservative aversion to such programs in the United States, however, transcends mere considerations of economic efficiency. Notions of personal and political freedom are closely linked in this country to notions of economic freedom and the concept of the 'free market' system, which is, in the popular mind, a hallmark of American society. Incomes policies, controls, and even guidelines are consequently looked upon as antithetical to the competitive and individual values of American society.

Neo-Keynesians and the Phillips Curve

Despite the apparently worsening trade-off between unemployment and inflation throughout the 1970s, a number of American economists rejected the implications of the rational expectations revolution. Although recognising that inflationary expectations affect the actual rate of inflation, the idea that expectations are both highly reliable and perfectly incorporated into wage bargains was specifically rejected. Thus, the notion of a long-run inflation/unemployment trade-off is retained, although the long-run Phillips curve is posited to be steeper than the short-run curve, that is, $c(2)$ in Equation 3 is hypothesized to be less than 1.0, but possibly substantially greater than 0.0.

Clearly in the vanguard of the Keynesian resurgence have been Arthur Okun, George Perry, and their associates at the Brookings Institution. Neo-Keynesian thought in the United States is marked by a greater sensitivity to theoretical considerations and model specification. This approach has incorporated arguments drawn from the institutionalist literature, particularly recent efforts to relate institutional processes to the neoclassical analysis of the labour market; of particular significance have been studies dealing with the operation of internal labour markets[14] and the market failure perspective.[15] The most ambitious statement of the neo-Keynesian perspective to date is Okun's posthumously-published work.[16] There have been a number of empirical studies undertaken from this perspective in recent years, most of which employ sophisticated statistical methods. These studies generally find an alternation of the wage-unemployment relationship in unionised settings and wage adjustment interdependencies with potential inflationary effects.[17]

WAGE POLICIES IN THE UNITED STATES

We now turn to a consideration of various incomes policy programmes, starting with the experiences of World War II. Although our concern is primarily with wage and pay policies, it is not possible, in the American context, to separate these from price restraint programmes. With few exceptions, price restraint has been implemented in conjunction with wage restraint measures. Thus, it is necessary to consider aspects of the price restraint programmes, as well as their wage restraint counterparts.

Wartime Policies
Although the United States was actively involved in World War I for less than two years, the mobilisa-tion effort led to price increases and distortions in the production of war materials. As the American labour movment was quite weak at the time, infla-tionary pressures were largely a product market, rather than labour market, phenomenon. However, formal price controls were not imposed. The War Industries Board negotiated prices with manufac-turers, but its power was rather limited. In gen-eral, the government's response to inflation was weak and ineffective, providing numerous oppor-tunities for profiteering.

Defense production increased substantially almost two years prior to American entry into the Second World War. Selective price controls were implemented under the authority of the Office of Price Administration by early 1941, though it was not until several months after Pearl Harbour that the general price controls were put in place.[18] Price controls were supplemented by the rationing of certain goods for the civilian population. Since the country was still recovering from the Depression in the early 1940s, inflationary pressures resulting from labour market shortages were initially minimal.

United States: Control in the Free Market

As mobilisation proceeded after December, 1941, such shortages began to have greater impact. Moreover, the dramatic rise of industrial unionism in the 1930s meant that institutional constraints on the functioning of the labour market associated with collective bargaining were prevalent, especially in basic manufacturing industries central to the war effort.

Although the Roosevelt administration secured a no-strike pledge from organised labour early on, it was apparent that some regulatory mechanism would be needed to deal with the realities of collective bargaining and labour shortages in what promised to be a protracted war effort. Consequently, the National War Labour Board was established. Initially the Board's power was limited to resolving impasses under collective bargaining; thus, voluntary wage increases in the non-union sector, as well as increases negotiated in the absence of an impasse, were not subject to Board approval. By late 1942, however, Board approval was required for virtually all wage increases. The Board developed what were seen to be non-inlationary standards, embodied in the so-called 'Little Steel' formula. Yet this standard - which aimed at restoring and maintaining real wages at January, 1941 levels - was not inflexible; exceptional cases resulted in Board approval of deviation from the standard. The Board was also concerned with preserving wage structures, as well as assuring adequate manpower flows to critical industries, though this was a less significant consideration. The effort during the war to control wages and prices is generally given high marks. In the first several months of the war, inflation was running at an annual rate of about 12%, but, after implementation of wage and price controls, that rate was cut to less than 5% for consumer prices and 3% for wages.[20] Controls were lifted after the cessation of hostilities. While wages and prices rose dramatically in the immediate post-war years, efforts by the Truman administration to reimpose controls were rejected by Congress.

The North Korean invasion of South Korea in 1950 and the subsequent United Nations sponsored 'police action' - essentially an American activity - were not viewed initially as major threats to wage and price stability. By this time, the rate of inflation had moderated considerably from the immediate post-war years and the scale of operations in Korea was not anticipated to tax excessively the

24

productive capacity of the economy. But initial
successes in the prosecution of the war were
reversed with the entry of China in November, 1950.
The Cold War mentality of the times and the general
paranoia in the country regarding the Soviet Union
evoked the spectre of World War III, fuelling inflationary pressures; the rate of change in the
consumer price index rose from 1% in 1949 to 7% in
1950. Consequently, a general freeze on wages and
prices was imposed in early 1951, with separate
agencies charged with establishing wage and price
standards and enforcing the controls. Wages were
under the jurisdiction of the Wage Stabilisation
Board (WSB), an eighteen-member tri-partite commission. Unlike the National War Labour Board in World
War II, the WSB had limited dispute resolution
powers and did not benefit from a no-strike pledge.
Moreover, there was considerable opposition to the
control programme. Congressional action limited the
authority of the Office of Price Stabilisation and
labour representatives on the WSB withdrew after the
imposition of a wage freeze. Enforcement of WSB
rulings was difficult at best, as perhaps best
illustrated by federal government seizure of steel
plants in 1952 after employers rejected a
WSB-determined settlement. With the control system
unpopular and peace clearly approaching, the Eisenhower administration, ideologically opposed to
controls in any event, quickly revoked them after
taking office in 1953.
     Despite controversy at the time, the Truman
controls do appear to have significantly reduced the
increases in consumer prices. Inflation rates in
1952 and 1953 averaged less than 2% and, unlike in
World War II, the termination of controls did not
lead to renewed inflation. Yet critics contend that
the controls were imposed too late and maintained
too long.[21] Serious distortions in wage and
price structures had already been created and were
maintained as a consequence of the controls. Moreover, though successful at limiting the rate of
inflation in consumer prices, wage inflation was
largely unchecked by the WSB, with wage increases
out-distancing price increases by several percentage
points during the control period.[22]

The Kennedy-Johnson Guidelines
By the late 1950s, most of those in national policy-
making positions appear to have at least implicitly
accepted the argument that inflationary pressures

could be created and perpetuated as the result of concentrations of market power. What was then perceived to be serious inflation began to reappear in the late 1950s, with the general price level rising at an average annual rate in excess of 2% between 1956 and 1960, as compared to a virtual absence of price inflation from 1952 to 1956. Renewed inflation became a serious political problem for the Eisenhower administration. The inflation persisted despite restrictive economic policies; although the government was opposed in principle to wage and price controls, there was popular support for such action. Given the realities of a wage-price spiral and a deepening recession, the administration promoted the doctrine of 'shared responsibility', which held that business and labour interests, particularly in key sectors, must exercise voluntary restraint in order to moderate inflation.[23] This approach involved presidential admonitions when wage settlements or pricing policies in such sectors were seen as inflationary. Evaluations of the Eisenhower approach are mixed, though considerable credit is given by many to the handling of the steel negotiations in 1959 and the ultimate mediation of the dispute by the Secretary of Labour and then Vice-President Nixon.

With John F. Kennedy's election to the presidency in 1960, American economic policy clearly entered a new era. The Council of Economic Advisers (CEA), headed by Walter Heller, formulated a series of policies intended to pull the economy out of recession. Unlike prior approaches, the 'new economics' of Heller and his associates was a direct application of Keynesian theory, culminating in the tax cut of 1964. Despite the ultimate triumph of the Keynesians, the earlier days of the Kennedy administration were not marked by consensus about the appropriate policies to generate economic recovery. Fiscal conservatives within the administration argued that economic recovery could best be promoted by improving the balance of payments picture and increasing American competitiveness in the world economy. For tactical, as well as philosophical, reasons, advocates of competing positions were able to agree early on that some system of wage and price restraint was desirable.[24] Reduced inflation, of course, was expected to improve the balance of payments and thus appealed to the conservatives; the Keynesians recognised that the excessive wage and price increases which might occur in key sectors in the early phases of a deficit-induced recovery could thwart that recovery.

Development of a viable wage and price policy was no simple matter and occupied several months. Although the possibility of mandatory controls was considered, such a draconian approach was seen to be unnecessary. Indeed, the programme was ultimately presented to the public as a system of wage and price guideposts, since the expression 'guideposts' was felt to convey a less coercive tone than 'guidelines.' In addition to being voluntary, there was concern that the policy be viewed as neutral with respect to labour and management interests and be generally applicable across the economy.[25] The policy that emerged[26] differed from the wartime controls both in terms of its voluntary nature and its emphasis on productivity as the criterion for evaluating wage increases and price adjustments. The guideposts called for wage increases that approximated the overall growth trend in labour productivity, measured by reference to output per man-hour. Thus, assuming the price adjustment process depicted in Equation (2), prices would tend to remain unchanged. The guideposts did anticipate a number of exceptions to this general rule. Prices in industries with less than average productivity gains would be expected to rise, while those in industries with higher than average productivity changes ought to fall; allowances were also made for surpluses or shortages of labour or capital in particular industries.[27] The CEA was not initially prepared to define trend productivity in precise quantitative terms. It first suggested a range of between 2.5% and 3.1%; starting in 1964, a point estimate of 3.2% was used.[28]

The first application of the guideposts came in late 1961 and early 1962 with the negotiation of contracts in both the automobile and basic steel industries. Both sets of negotiations were critical since these settlements were widely regarded as the major pattern-setting settlements in the economy. Moreover, price inflation in steel, a basic ingredient in so many other products, could result in a general upward pressure on prices throughout the economy. The administration succeeded in persuading both the United Automobile Workers and the United Steelworkers to negotiate wage provisions well within the guidepost limits. However, the resolve of the administration was soon tested; despite a 2.5% wage settlement in steel, the major producers shortly thereafter announced price increases in the

range of 3.5%. This presented a direct threat to
the integrity of the guideposts, as well as a direct
challenge to the authority of the President. The
administration, of course, could not mandate a price
rollback, since neither a price freeze nor controls
had been imposed. The steel companies claimed that
below trend productivity and low profits justified
the industry's departure from the guideposts. Yet
Kennedy and his advisers were able to focus considerable pressure on the steel firms rapidly,
resulting in an almost immediate decision by the
steel companies to roll back prices to pre-existing
levels.[29]

The first year of the guideposts witnessed at
least short-term success for the Kennedy administration; two key contracts had been negotiated within
guidepost limits and steel prices had been contained. However, the steel case raised some dis-
quieting questions regarding the viability of the
programme. With voluntary guideposts, there was no
elaborate administrative system to monitor wages and
prices and enforce rules, as under controls. If
parties wilfully ignored the guideposts, as in the
case of the steel manufacturers, then public scrutiny, which had been intended as the primary enforcement mechanism, apparently was ineffective.
Yet the President could not be expected to intervene
in each and every crisis. Alternative enforcement
means were considered, including legislation that
would allow the President to petition the federal
courts for a temporary injunction to stop price
increases seen to be 'inimical to the public
welfare.'[30] Concern with inflation as a primary
economic problem, however, was at least temporarily
deflected in the 1962-64 period by continuing high
unemployment - approximately 6% - which clearly
moderated most wage and price increases.[31] The
inflation rate in this period ran only around 1% and
many argue that economic conditions, not the guideposts, explain this.

The guidepost approach clearly began to unravel
in 1965 and, by 1967, the guideposts were effectively abandoned. The 1964 tax reduction, coupled with
escalating American involvement in Vietnam, led to
substantial reductions in unemployment and increasing levels of production. Tight market conditions generated increasing wholesale and, ultimately, consumer prices. While the Johnson administration met with some success in limiting certain price
increases, evaluations of this effort are mixed and
the effects appear to have been largely

symbolic.[32] A number of major wage settlements
in 1965 and 1966 significantly exceeded the guidepost standard of 3.2%. In a statement issued in
1966, the leading American labour organisation, the
American Federation of Labour - Congress of Industrial Organisations (AFL-CIO), criticised the guideposts for not taking into account inflation in
establishing wage standards.[33] In fact, much of
the inflationary pressure with regard to wages
emanated from the largely unorganised service sector
as a consequence of tightening labour markets. The
guideposts were not intended to deal with such
widely-dispersed wage inflation forces, which were
really demand-pull rather than cost-push in
character. Another important source of wage
inflation was unionised contract construction. The
highly decentralised nature of collective bargaining
in construction in the United States made monitoring
of wage settlements in the industry by the CEA and
the President impossible, though settlements in the
industry were running in excess of 10% in many
cases. Hence, by 1967, the guideposts retained
little, if any, credibility. The administration
considered a variety of alternatives, including
all-out controls, but these were never implemented.
Eventually, Johnson established the Cabinet
Committee on Price Stability (CCPS). Although
initially charged with enforcing wage and price
standards, the CCPS also attempted to effect change
by persuasion, through 'jawboning,' identifying wage
and price increases seen to be especially
inflationary.[34] However, an explicit standard,
such as that set forth in the guideposts, was not
used in this effort.
     How, then, are we to evaluate the guidepost
era? Econometric studies suggest that the guideposts reduced wage inflation from between .7 to 1.7
percentage points,[35] though specification and
measurement problems raise questions as to the
reliabilty of these figures. It has been suggested
that a similar effect occurred in the case of
prices.[36] Despite the statistical findings, a
number of questions remain regarding the political
success of the guideposts. The charge that they
were unfair in that the CEA focused on highly
visible wage settlements and price changes in key
sectors is often voiced, though a contrary argument
may be raised that such discriminatory application
is an unavoidable and desirable aspect of guidelines. The guidepost programme was continually
plagued by objections to its relatively fixed

standard, which was seen to prevent it being as res-
ponsive as it should have been to the particular
circumstances of various sectors of the economy.[37]
Dunlop identifies several flaws with the programme,
including a failure by the administration to achieve
widespread public input and support for the guideposts.[38]   He is also troubled by the abstract
nature of the productivity concept which he argues
to be difficult to implement at the micro level.

The Nixon Controls

After assuming power in 1969, the Nixon administration unequivocally rejected whatever vestiges
remained of the Kennedy-Johnson guidepost programme.
The rate of inflation in 1968 had been just under 5%
- the highest since the pre-control period of the
Korean War.   However, the inflation was not attributed to cost-push pressures. A burgeoning federal
deficit, occasioned by the deepening American involvement in Vietnam and a variety of anti-poverty
programmes at home, had generated a shortfall in the
federal budget of $25 billion in 1968 - far out-
pacing any previous deficit since the Second World
War. As already noted, inflationary pressures were
perhaps strongest in weakly organised and relatively
competitive sectors.   Thus, demand-pull pressures
were seen as the principal culprit. Nixon's economic advisers argued strongly that guidelines and controls served only to distort market processes.   The
programme pursued in the first couple of years of
the Nixon administration consequently emphasised the
use of fiscal and monetary instruments to reduce the
deficit and quell inflationary expectations.[39]
Although these policies did lead to a substantially
reduced budget deficit and a reduction in the rate
of growth in the money supply, the rate of inflation
continued to rise. The restrictive economic policies also led to a sharp increase in the unemployment rate, from 3.5% in 1969 to 5.9% in 1971.

By late 1971, the persistence of high inflation
coupled with high unemployment began to condition
those within the administration to accept some type
of incomes policy. Two explanations were presented
for the apparent failure of the existing policies to
curb inflation.[40]   First, significant lags in
inflationary expectations, resulting from a protracted inflationary episode, meant that fiscal and
monetary policies would take longer to work than
originally anticipated.   Second, cost-push pressures, associated with collective bargaining and

pricing policies in concentrated industries, were thwarting policy objectives. The transition to wage-price controls was not immediate. The President engaged in some 'jawboning' efforts in 1970 and 1971 and was able to obtain some significant price rollbacks. The Council of Economic Advisers began issuing 'inflation alerts,' periodic reports identifying potentially inflationary wage settlements and price increases. These initiatives, however, had only limited impact.

Inflation in the construction industry was reaching crisis proportions by early 1971. The strong upswing in the economy in the late 1960s had led to upward pressure on wages in this heavily unionised sector. The structure of bargaining in construction in the United States is complex and highly decentralised, with nearly twenty different craft unions negotiating several thousand local and regional contracts. This decentralisation, coupled with the tradition of maintaining intercraft and inter-area differentials, generated strong wage 'spillover' pressures in the industry, leading to cost-push inflation. With wage settlements exceeding 15% and 20% in many cases, construction became the target of the first wage restraint programme of the Nixon administration. Under the programme, implemented by an executive order of the President in March, 1971, all negotiated wage increases in contract construction were required to be approved by the tri-partite Construction Industry Stabilisation Committee (CISC). Criteria used by the CISC included productivity gains in construction and changes in the cost of living. However, unlike the Kennedy-Johnson guideposts, CISC explicitly took into account wage differentials and often allowed substantial deviations from standards in order to re-establish or preserve such differentials.

Continued stagnation in the economy and an inflation rate apparently unresponsive to recessionary conditions generated continued pressure for presidential action in other sectors of the economy. With national elections little more than a year off, the administration felt it necessary to stimulate the economy and limit the potential for such actions simply to translate into additional wage and price increases. Consequently, Nixon and his advisers felt the need for an incomes policy. Believing voluntary guidelines and 'jawboning' to have been discredited by the experiences of the 1960s, the administration developed a incomes policy programme that departed dramatically from its early policies.

United States: Control in the Free Market

Nixon's 'New Economic Policy,' as it came to be known, commenced with a general freeze on wages, prices, and rents that was imposed on August 15, 1971 (Phase I). The Freeze was replaced 90 days later by the Phase II control programme. The seven-member Price Commission was created to enforce regulations relating to price and rent increases; wage increases were subject to the control of the tri-partite Pay Board, which consisted of a total of 15 labour, employer, and public representatives. Construction wages continued to be regulated by CISC. The entire control programme was co-ordinated by the cabinet-level Cost-of-Living Council (CLC), chaired by the Secretary of the Treasury.

The policies of the Pay Board were tied to the overall inflation rate goals developed by the CLC and implemented by the Pay Commission. Recognizing the need for some slack, that standard was set at approximately 2.5%; allowing for a 3% annual rate of increase in productivity, the Pay Board established a 5.5% annual rate as the standard for wage increases.[41] Exceptions to the standard were allowed under a restricted set of circumstances, though even exceptional cases were limited to a maximum wage increase of 7%. Unlike the Wage Stabilisation Board of the 1950s or the National War Labour Board of the 1940s, the Pay Board did not become involved in the resolution of labour disputes; rather, its function was limited to establishing and interpreting rules relating to wage increase.

The initial policies of the Pay Board were unfavourably received by organised labour as a consequence of the manner in which increases negotiated under existing contracts were treated. Such deferred increases, were, in general, disallowed if they exceeded the 5.5% standard. Unions also objected to the treatment of fringe benefits in the formula used to calculate wage increases. As a result of union pressure, Congress, while extending the Economic Stabilisation Act which authorised the President to establish controls, imposed certain restrictions on Pay Board policies relating to these and some other issues. Within these limits, the Pay Board developed a complex set of policies relating to a wide range of matters.[42] However, labour's discontent with Pay Board actions continued and, in March, 1972, three of the four labour representatives on the Board resigned. The Pay Board was then reconstituted with all public members and continued to function until the Phase III programme was implemented in 1973.

The control programme, coupled with an expansionary economic policy, led to a substantial recovery in 1972 and 1973. The annual rate of inflation for 1972 was down to 3.5% - only moderately higher than the objective - and the unemployment rate, though slow to respond initially, began to drop to what many argued was its natural rate. Consequently, controls were significantly relaxed in early 1973. Under Phase III, both the Pay Board and Price Commission were abolished (though CISC was retained) and the remaining functions of these agencies were assumed by the CLC. With regard to wages, Phase III was concerned primarily with limiting inflationary key unit increases. Thus, large segments of the economy were effectively removed from direct wage controls, though the programme nominally survived through 'self-administered' controls. The argument given for the relaxation was that anti-inflation goals were being achieved and that continued enforcement costs were unwarranted.[43] It also appears that opposition to the agencies created political incentives for their termination.[44]

By mid-1973, inflationary pressures began to reappear.[45] Demand-pull forces associated with the rapidly expanding economy, both here and abroad, impacted on wages and prices. Although controls were still nominally in place, they were frequenty ignored. More importantly, 1973 saw the first of a series of supply shocks that were to plague the economy for much of the rest of the decade. Poor harvests led to dramatic food price increases, raw material shortages spurred price increases in the world market, and the actions of the major oil-producing nations led to sharp increases in petroleum prices. The supply shocks led to a foundering of the economy and double-digit inflation rates coexisting with unemployment rates of around 8%. The administration responded by first strengthening the Phase III controls with respect to prices, then imposing a 60-day freeze on prices during the summer of 1973; the freeze was followed by Phase IV of the control programme, essentially a continuation of Phase III.[46] However, neither the freeze nor Phase IV imposed any new restrictions on wages, although some limitations on executive compensation were initiated. The administration, preoccupied with the Watergate scandal and generally dubious regarding the effectiveness of controls under existing economic conditions, did not seek

continuation of control authority after the expira-
tion of the Economic Stabilisation Act in April,
1974; political and popular support for the programme was also lacking.[47]   Hence, the controls
were allowed to lapse.

Evaluating the effectiveness of the Nixon
controls in moderating inflationary pressures,
particularly with respect to wages, is difficult,
though a number of studies have been published.
Initially, the earlier stages of the programme
(Phases I and II) appear to have had a substantial
impact on wage and price inflation.   Gordon[48]
found that, at least in the first several months of
the Nixon programme, wage inflaton was reduced by
about .7% and price inflation by almost 2%.   He
further argues that, as a consequence of this
reduction, unemployment was significantly less by
mid-1972 than would have been the case in the
absence of controls.   Other studies, however, have
found no significant impact associated with either
the wage or price controls.[49]   Mitchell and
Azevedo[50] examined the impact of wage and price
controls on various market phenomena other than wage
and price changes.   Although they found that price
controls had some distorting effects on product
markets, they were unable to discern any distortions
in labour market performance attributable to the
wage controls.

Studies of the impact of the controls on construction wages, administered by CISC, are somewhat
more conclusive.   Mills[51] observed a direct,
negative impact on construction wage settlements
attributable to CISC controls.   Extending that
analysis, Ross[52] found CISC controls depressed
wage settlements in construction by between 3% and
5%, with a significant portion of this effect being
the result of dampened spillover pressures.

The Carter Guidelines
Fiscal and monetary policy steps taken in 1975 and
1976 led to a strong recovery that continued through
the end of the decade.   However, unemployment
remained relatively high, despite increasing real
output.   Moreover, inflation, which had dipped below
the double-digit levels of 1974 and 1975 in 1976,
began accelerating in 1977.   As real earnings began
eroding, the newly-elected Carter administration
considered steps to contain inflation.   The position
of Carter's advisers regarding inflationary momentum
in the economy was that the institutional

characteristics of the economy, particularly the
highly concentrated and organised sectors, introduced rigidities and insensitivities to market
conditions; hence, inflationary pressures, once in
place, were not readily dampened by demand management techniques.[53] Declining productivity
growth and exogenous material price shocks were also
seen as important inflationary pressures. Wage and
price guidelines were developed in order to reduce
inflation, especially in the less competitive
sectors.

At first, employers and unions were asked to
limit wage and price increases to a level below
average increases in the preceding two years. The
general ambiguity of the standard resulted in
limited compliance. Hence, formal, but voluntary,
wage and price guidelines were introduced in
October, 1978. Although price increase standards
were laid out in the Carter programme, these were
rather diffuse and the principal focus of the
program was the containment of wage inflation. The
rather involved standard aimed at limiting average
wage and salary increases to 7% annually. As with
past programmes, there were numerous exceptions to
allow the programme to be sufficiently flexible.[54] In order to win support for the programme, especially from a dubious labour movement,
the Carter administration proposed a 'real wage
insurance' programme.

Based on the more general notion of tax-based
incomes policies (TIP),[55] the plan called for
tax rebates, should inflation exceed the 7% wage
standard, for all employees in firms in compliance
with the wage standard. Thus, if a given employee
received a wage increase less than or equal to 7%
and the actual rate of inflation for the year was,
say, 9%, then he or she would receive a tax credit
equal to 2% of his or her wages, representing actual
inflation minus the standard. The TIP approach was
never implemented because of Congressional
opposition and the unenthusiastic reaction to the
proposal by organised labour. The idea of a real
wage insurance programme has been criticised on
several counts, and its implementation would have
created serious administrative difficulties.[56]

There appears to have been reasonable compliance with the wage standard in the first year of the
programme, despite the failure of the administration
in securing passage of the real wage guarantee. The
methods used in assessing compliance, however, led
to serious equity problems as a result of the

substantial increase in oil and other raw materials prices in 1979. A high proportion of union contracts in the United States contain cost-of-living adjustment (COLA) clauses. In assessing compliance with the wage standard, the administration assumed a 6% rate of inflation for 1979, so that contracts with expected increases of 7% or less, based on actual increases and estimated contingent increases (given 6% inflation), were determined to be in compliance with the wage standard. Unfortunately, the actual rate of inflation reached about 11% in 1979, resulting in substantially greater than expected increases for wages protected by COLA provisions. Inflationary pressures were thus magnified and COLA-protected workers enjoyed a clear advantage over those not protected by COLA provisions, most frequently non-unionised employees.

The programme confronted serious difficulties as wage and price standards were reviewed in the latter part of 1979. The ever-increasing gap between the wages of unionised and non-unionised workers, now fuelled by the treatment of COLA clauses under the wage-price programme, threatened to reduce compliance by non-union firms concerned about the increasing attractiveness of unions to their employees because of this gap; organised labour remained ambivalent about the programme; and efforts to obtain passage of the real wage insurance pro- posal appeared pointless. In order to salvage the programme, the Carter administration succeeded in persuading the labour leadership in the AFL-CIO to agree to a general programme of action to reduce inflation and promote economic growth. The agreement, termed the 'National Accord,' was intended as something of a European-style social contract. Unfortunately, the complex and decentralised nature of bargaining in the United States and the failure of the administration to include business representatives in these discussions rendered the document virtually irrelevant.[57]

Inflationary pressures intensified in 1980 despite the continuing wage-price programme. The administration estimated that wage increases were 1% to 1.5% less than would have been the case without the pay standards.[58] Nonetheless, inflation reached nearly 14% by 1980, a factor which clearly contributed to Carter's defeat by Ronald Reagan in November of that year. The Reagan administration promptly withdrew the standards and embarked on its own 'supply-side' approach to containing inflation.

United States: Control in the Free Market

AN ASSESSMENT OF AMERICAN POLICY

The literature dealing with income policy in the
United States is extensive and this chapter is nec-
essarily limited in terms of the issues examined and
studies referenced. Despite a general aversion to
the intrusion of government into wage and price
setting processes, America has had considerable experience with wage-price restraint programmes. The
reviews of these experiments are, however, mixed at
best. Most programmes were plagued by discord and
conflict and recent efforts are popularly viewed as
having failed. In concluding this examination of
American policy, I shall focus on three fairly
general issues: the impact of guidelines and controls on the economy, the administrative and political difficulties associated with conducting such
programmes, and the applicability of such programmes
given current conditions in the American economy.

The Impact of Wage and Price Policies
Evidence regarding the impact of guidelines and
controls is mixed and often difficult to interpret.
The wartime control programmes have typically been
evaluated by qualitative and non-rigorous quantitative methods. For the most part, these programmes
are given relatively high marks for limiting inflation, especially the policies used during World
War II. More recent efforts have been evaluated by
means of fairly rigorous statistical techniques. By
and large, these studies suggest that both pay and
price standards have limited, short-run effects,
resulting in inflation which is lower than expected
and in improved economic performance. In the long
term, however, the policies seem to fail in the face
of excess demand pressures, exogenous price shocks,
and administrative difficulties. Moreover, when the
policies are lifted, accumulated demand may over-
compensate for diminished inflation during the
period of restraint. These programmes may also lead
to longer-term distortions in structural relationships within the economy, as, for example, occurred
as a consequence of the treatment of COLA provisions
during the Carter programme.
     The verdict, then, appears to be unfavourable,
at least with regard to traditional economic policy
methods. Short-term programmes in response to endo-
genous cost-push pressures may be warranted in extreme circumstances, though on-going programmes, except in times of national crisis, are apt to fail.

United States: Control in the Free Market

Political and Administrative Issues
The central issue in any wage-price restraint programme is the development of a set of criteria by
which wage increases and price adjustments can be
assessed in terms of inflationary potential. American programmes have normally opted for a general
standard. The wage standard is usually based on
general increases in productivity or the cost of
living, or both, with the price standard allowing
for the pass-through of labour cost increases minus
productivity gains. General wage and price standards are problematic, however, in that they are
often difficult to interpret in operational terms by
economic decision-makers. In the highly decentralised American economy, general standards often
lead to serious distortions in wage and price
structures,[59] thus disrupting the allocative
functions of the market and collective bargaining
activities. Consequently, most programmes have
allowed for at least some exceptions to the
standards; there have been experiments with the
creation of specific agencies to oversee programmes
in particular sectors of the economy, as with the
CISC in the construction industry.

Programmes that allowed considerable flexibility in adapting standards to special circumstances
have tended to be more successful than those which
have relied on a single, relatively inflexible
standard. Unfortunately, flexible standards are
associated with significantly higher administrative
costs. The wartime control programmes, as well as
Phase II of the Nixon programme, employed relatively
flexible standards, along with large administrative
staffs which monitored compliance and examined cases
for exceptions to the standards. All three programmes had separate wage and price agencies, as
well as a central co-ordinating body.[60]

In addition to the direct costs of supporting
bureaucratic machinery to administer the programme,
we must also account for the administrative costs to
the private sector associated with establishing
compliance with controls. Given the general tendency in the United States toward deregulation and
reductions in the size of government, it is unlikely
that such an elaborate and complex regulatory apparatus will be established again in the foreseeable
future. For the reasons discussed above, self-
administered controls, such as tax-based incomes
policies, are also unlikely to garner much public
support.

Another major issue in the implementation of a

38

restraint programme is the choice of using mandatory controls versus voluntary guidelines. The empirical data suggest that guidelines may be no less effective than controls. Guidelines are certainly less costly to administer. However, guidelines have never been purely voluntary in the United States. The President has often used the power of his office to impose, or threaten, economic and political sanctions on highly visible firms and unions which flout the guidelines. The on-going coercion often necessary to make guidelines work may become a political liability for the President and become costly in terms of the competing demands imposed on his time. This, of course, was a major difficulty with the Kennedy-Johnson guideposts.

Finally, embarking on an incomes policy is as much a political as an economic intervention in private affairs; it is necesary to build and maintain a consensus of support among representatives of key sectors of the economy. This requires, especially in the case of pay restraint, the co-operation of both labour and management. Control programmes have normally relied on tri-partite boards to achieve this co-operation, but these boards have frequently been characterised by internal conflict, with representatives of one faction or another withdrawing membership. Indeed, the pluralistic nature of American politics and the traditionally adversarial nature of union-management relations in this country make establishing long-term support by both labour unions and management virtually impossible. And even if that were not the case, the decentralisation of bargaining, as well as price-setting, in many key sectors of the economy, render any high-level agreements to co-operate on an incomes policy - as in the case of the social contract - relatively weak as instruments in achieving broad consensus.

The Future of Incomes Policies in the United States
It appears extremely unlikely that we will see anything smacking of a formal incomes policy in the United States in the forseeable future. In general, wage and price restraint programmes, at least those with any clout, are unpopular and, for the various reasons suggested above, politically unacceptable. The Reagan administration, which took office in 1981, has embarked on an aggressive, though not always consistent and well-articulated, economic programme based on the supply-side and rational

39

expectations perspectives.

Inflation was an extremely important issue in the 1980 election and the Reagan administration has clearly demonstrated that disinflation by means of monetary and fiscal policy can achieve that objective. By mid-1986, the rate of inflation for the consumer price index was running at about 4%, a sharp drop from the double-digit levels that plagued the Carter administration. Wage inflation is even lower, particularly among unionised employees. What has come to be known as 'concession bargaining' in the United States - the practice of unions accepting wage cuts or the elimination of long-standing contract provisions - is common in a wide variety of industries. Thus, the argument that unions create strong downward rigidities in wages necessitating wage restraint programmes appears to be invalid when economic conditions are sufficiently severe. American unions have experienced a substantial decline in power and influence over the past 20 years. Thus, even in the absence of the Reagan policies, there has been a tendency toward less insulated labour markets.

FOOTNOTES

1. Phillips, A.W., 'The Relation Between Unemployment and the Rate of Change in Money Wage Rates in the United Kingdom, 1861-1957,' Economica, vol. 25 (November, 1958).

2. Lipsey, Richard G., 'The Relation Between Unemployment and the Rate of Change in Money Wage Rates in the United Kingdom 1862-1957: A Further Analysis,' Economica, vol. 27 (February, 1960).

3. Samuelson, Paul A., and Robert M. Solow, 'Analytical Aspects of Anti-Inflation Policy,' Papers and Proceedings of the American Economic Association, vol. 50 (May, 1960), pp. 308-315.

4. Perry, George, Unemployment, Money Wage Rates and Inflation (MIT Press, Cambridge, Mass., 1966).

5. Dunlop, John, 'The Task of Contemporary Wage Theory,' in J. Dunlop (ed.) The Theory of Wage Determination, (MacMillan, London, 1966), pp. 3-30.

6. Livernash, E. Robert, 'Wages and Benefits,' in G. Somers (ed.), A Review of Industrial Relations Research, vol. I (Industrial Relations Research Association, Madison, Wis., 1970), pp. 79-145.

7. See, for example, Eckstein, Otto and Thomas Wilson, 'The Determination of Money Wages in American Industry,' Quarterly Journal of Economics,

vol. 76 (1968), pp. 379-414.

8. Garbarino, Joseph, Wage Policy and Long-Term Contracts (Brookings Institution, Washington, D.C., 1962).

9. Phelps, Edmund, 'Phillips Curves, Expectations of Inflation, and Optimal Unemployment over Time,' Economica, vol. 34 (1967), pp. 254-261.

10. Friedman, Milton, 'The Role of Monetary Policy,' American Economic Review, vol. 58 (1968), pp. 7-11.

11. Phelps, Edmund (ed.), Microeconomic Foundations of Employment and Inflation Theory (Norton, New York, 1970).

12. Mortenson, Dale, 'Theory of Wage and Unemployment Dynamics,' in ibid., pp. 167-211.

13. Gordon, Robert, 'Recent Developments in the Theory of Inflation and Unemployment,' Journal of Monetary Economics, vol. 2 (1976), pp. 185-219.

14. Doeringer, Peter and Michael Piore, Internal Labour Markets (Heath-Lexington, Lexington, Ma., 1971).

15. Williamson, Oliver, Markets and Hierarchies: Analysis and Antitrust Implications (Free Press, New York, 1975).

16. Okun, Arthur, Prices and Quantities: A Macroeconomic Analysis (Brookings Institution, Washington, D.C., 1980).

17. See, for example, Mitchell, Daniel J.B., Unions, Wages and Inflation (Brookings Institution, Washington, D.C., 1980).

18. Ross, Arthur, 'Guideline Policy - Where We Are and How We Got There,' in Schultz, George and Robert Aliber (eds.), Guidelines, Informal Controls and the Market Place (University of Chicago Press, Chicago, 1966), pp. 97-142.

19. Mills, Daniel Quinn, Government, Labor and Inflation (University of Chicago Press, Chicago, 1975), pp. 150-152.

20. Ross, 'Guideline Policy.'

21. Ibid.

22. Mills, Government, Labor and Inflation, p. 36.

23. Gordon, 'Recent Developments.'

24. Barber, William, 'The Kennedy Years: Purposeful Pedagogy,' in Goodwin, Crawford (ed.), Exhortation and Controls: The Search for a Wage-Price Policy 1945-1971 (Brookings Institution, Washington, D.C., 1975), pp. 135-192.

25. Ibid.

26. Economic Report of the President (Government Printing Office, Washington, D.C., 1962), pp.

185-190.
27. Ibid., p. 189.
28. Economic Report of the President (Government Printing Office, Washington, D.C., 1964), pp. 112-116.
29. Sheahan, John, The Wage-Price Guideposts (Brookings Institution, Washington, D.C., 1967), pp. 33-38.
30. Barber, 'The Kennedy Years.'
31. Sheahan, The Wage-Price Guideposts, pp. 33-43.
32. Ibid., pp. 62-78.
33. Ross, 'Guideline Policy.'
34. Cochrane, James G., 'The Johnson Administration: Moral Suasion Goes to War,' in Goodwin (ed.), Exhortation and Controls, pp. 193-296.
35. Gordon, Robert, 'Wage-Price Controls and the Shifting Phillips Curve,' Brookings Papers on Economic Activity (Brookings Institution, Washington, D.C., 1972), pp. 385-430.
36. Solow, Robert M., 'The Case Against the Case Against Guideposts,' in Schultz and Aliber (eds.), Guidelines, pp. 41-54.
37. Mills, Government, Labor and Inflation, pp. 43-44.
38. Dunlop, 'The Task.'
39. DeMarchi, Neil, 'The First Nixon Administration: Prelude to Controls,' in Goodwin (ed.), Exhortation and Controls, pp. 295-352.
40. Economic Report of the President (Government Printing Office, Washington, D.C., 1971), pp. 82-95.
41. Economic Report of the President (Government Printing Office, Washington, D.C., 1972), pp. 82-95.
42. Mills, Government, Labor and Inflation, pp. 54-65.
43. Economic Report of the President (Government Printing Office, Washington, D.C., 1973), pp. 78-82.
44. Mills, Government, Labor and Inflation, pp. 67-69.
45. Dornbusch, Rudiger and Stanley Fischer, Macroeconomics (McGraw-Hill, New York, 1981), pp. 570-573.
46. Economic Report of the President (Government Printing Office, Washington, D.C., 1974), pp. 88-104.
47. Economic Report of the President (Government Printing Office, Washington, D.C., 1975), pp. 223-229.

United States: Control in the Free Market

48. Gordon, 'Wage-Price Controls.'
49. Draft, Arthur, John Kraft and Blaine Roberts, 'An Alternative to Wage and Price Controls,' in Kraft, John and Blaine Roberts (eds.), Wage and Price Controls: The U.S. Experiment (Praeger, New York, 1975), pp. 80-95; Guy, Charles, John Kraft and Blaine Roberts, 'An Industrial Examination of Wage and Price Controls,' in Kraft and Roberts (eds.), Wage and Price Controls, pp. 96-115.
50. Mitchell, Daniel J.B. and Ross Azevedo, Wage-Price Controls and Labor-Market Distortions, (University of California Los Angeles Institute of Industrial Relations, Los Angeles, 1976).
51. Mills, Daniel Quinn, 'Explaining Pay Increases in Construction: 1953-1972,' Industrial Relations, vol. 13 (1974), pp. 196-201.
52. Ross, Clark, 'The Construction Wage Stabilization Program,' Industrial Relations, vol. 17 (1978), pp. 308-315.
53. Economic Report of the President (Government Printing Office, Washington, D.C., 1978), pp. 142-149.
54. Economic Report of the President (Government Printing Office, Washington, D.C., 1979), pp. 80-85.
55. Wallich, Henry and Sidney Weintraub, 'A Tax-Based Incomes Policy,' Journal of Economic Issues, vol. 5 (1971), p. 2; Seidman, Laurence, 'Tax-Based Incomes Policies,' in Brookings Papers on Economic Activity (Brookings Institution, Washington, D.C., 1978), pp. 301-362.
56. Mitchell, Daniel J.B., 'The Rise and Fall of Real Wage Insurance,' Industrial Relations, vol. 19 (1980), pp. 64-73.
57. Flanagan, Robert, 'The National Accord as a Social Contract,' Industrial and Labor Relations Review, vol. 34 (1980), pp. 35-48.
58. Economic Report of the President (Government Printing Office, Washington, D.C., 1981), p. 59.
59. Mills, Government, Labor and Inflation, pp. 149-211.
60. Derber, Milton, 'The Wage Stabilization Program in Historical Perspective,' Labor Law Journal, vol. 23 (1972), pp. 453-461.

REFERENCES

Derber, Milton, 'The Wage Stabilization Program in Historical Perspective,' Labor Law Journal, vol. 23 (1972), pp. 453-461.

Doeringer, Peter and Michael Piore, Internal Labour Markets (Heath-Lexington, Lexington, Ma. 1971).

Dornbusch, Rudiger and Stanley Fischer, Macro-economics (McGraw-Hill, New York, 1981).

Dunlop, John, (ed), The Theory of Wage Determination (MacMillan, London, 1966).

Eckstein, Otto and Thomas Wilson, 'The Determination of Money Wages in American Industry', Quarterly Journal of Economics, vol. 76 (1968), pp. 379-414.

Economic Report of the President (Government Printing Office, Washington, D.C., various years).

Flanagan, Robert, 'The National Accord as a Social Contract', Industrial and Labour Relations Review, vol. 34 (1980), pp. 35-48.

Friedman, Milton, The Role of Monetary Policy,' American Economic Review, vol. 58 (1968), pp. 7-11.

Garbarino, Joseph, Wage Policy and Long-Term Contracts, (Brookings Institution, Washington, D.C., 1962).

Goodwin, Crawford (ed.), Exhortation and Controls: The Search for a Wage-Price Policy 1945-1971 (Brookings Institution, Washington, D.C. 1975).

Gordon, Robert, 'Recent Developments in the Theory of Inflation and Unemployment', Journal of Monetary Economics, vol 2 (1976), pp. 185-219.

Gordon, Robert, 'Wage-Price Controls and the Shifting Phillips Curve', Brookings Papers on Economic Activity (Brookings Institution, Washington, D.C. 1972), pp. 385-430.

Kraft, John and Blaine Roberts (eds.) Wage and Price Controls: The U.S. Experiment (Praeger, New York, 1975).

Lipsey, Richard G., 'The Relation Between Unemployment and the Rate of Change of Money Wage Rates in the United Kingdom 1862-1957: A Further Analysis' Economica, vol. 27 (February, 1960).

Mills, Daniel Quinn, 'Explaining Pay Increases in Construction: 1953-1972,' Industrial Relations, vol. 13 (1974), pp. 196-201.

Mills, Daniel Quinn, Government, Labor and Inflation (University of Chicago Press, Chicago, 1975).

Mitchell, Daniel J.B., 'The Rise and Fall of Real Wage Insurance', Industrial Relations, vol. 19

(1980), pp. 64-73.

Mitchell, Daniel J.B., Unions, Wages and Inflation (Brookings Institution, Washington, D.C., (1980).

Mitchell, Daniel J.B. and Ross Azevedo, Wage-Price Controls and Labor Market Distortions (University of California Los Angeles Institute of Industrial Relations, Los Angeles, 1976).

Okun, Arthur, Prices and Quantities: A Macroeconomic Analysis (Brookings Institution, Washington, D.C., 1980).

Perry, George, Unemployment, Money Wage Rates and Inflation (MIT Press, Cambridge, Mass., 1966).

Phelps, Edmund (ed.), Microeconomic Foundations of Employment and Inflation Theory, (Norton, New York, 1970).

Phelps, Edmund, 'Phillips Curves, Expectations of Inflation and Optimal Unemployment Over Time,' Economica, vol. 34 (1967), pp. 254-261.

Ross, Clark, 'The Construction Wage Stabilization Program,' Industrial Relations, vol. 17 (1978), pp. 308-315.

Samuelson, Paul A. and Robert M. Solow, 'Analytical Aspects of Anti-Inflation Policy,' Papers and Proceedings of the American Economic Association, vol. 50 (May, 1960), pp. 308-315.

Schultz, George and Robert Aliber (eds.), Guidelines, Informal Controls and the Market Place (University of Chicago Press, Chicago, 1966).

Seidman, Lawrence, 'Tax-Based Incomes Policies', Brookings Papers on Economic Activity (Brookings Institution, Washington, D.C., 1978), pp. 301-362.

Sheahan, John, The Wage-Price Guideposts (Brookings Institution, Washington, D.C., 1967).

Somers, G. (ed.), A. Review of Industrial Relations Research, vol. I (Industrial Relations Research Association, Madison, Wis., 1970).

Wallich, Henry and Sidney Weintraub, 'A Tax-Based Incomes Policy', Journal of Economic Issues, vol. 5 (1971).

Williamson, Oliver, Markets and Hierarchies: Analysis of Antitrust Implications (Free Press, New York, 1975).

Chapter Two

GREAT BRITAIN: A SEEDBED OF POLICY OPTIONS

Beth Bilson

INTRODUCTION

Though each of the countries here surveyed takes its
unique place in the heroic struggle against
inflation which has been unfolding since the Second
World War, there can be few countries where as wide
a range of theories and devices have been tried,
where Keynesianism and its cousins took such hold,
or where neo-conservative economic policies have
been so insistently pursued, as in Great Britain.
      From 1945 till roughly 1979, succeeding
governments of both parties in Britain attempted to
use the instruments prescribed by Keynesian
principles to deal with the pressures arising from
inflation, demand for social benefits, industrial
decline and calls for full employment. Labour and
Conservative governments were, of course, subject to
differing political influences; they tended to see
things differently, and they articulated policy
goals which varied widely. Nonetheless, whatever
differences there were in emphasis on subjects like
economic planning, the role of the trade unions, or
the objectives of monetary and fiscal policy, there
were certain cornerstone assumptions from which
governments of either party never strayed too far.
The most important of these assumptions for our
purposes were that full employment is a desirable
social goal, that the apparatus of the welfare state
might be modified but not dismantled, and that the
existence of trade unions is an inevitable, and
perhaps useful, component of economic activity.
      In the mid-1970s, the intractability of
recession as a phenomenon of the British economy,
and the sudden spurts of inflation which occurred in
1973 and 1974,[1] among other things, led even
Labour politicians to question the optimistic

predictions of the Keynesians, and to find attractive the tenets of supply-side and monetarist economic theory. Though the election of a Conservative government committed to neo-conservative economic principles represents a convenient - and indeed important - turning point in economic policies, it should not be supposed that there was an absolute discontinuity.

A HISTORICAL SURVEY

This chapter will discuss briefly the various mechanisms which have been adopted since the war to control wages and then to consider the social implications of different approaches.

The Early Post-War Period
The measures taken by the Labour government after the hard winter of 1947 were not initially conceived as the opening shots of the war against inflation. Rather they were viewed as a temporary expedient to assist in the post-war recovery of the economy, and to prevent an undesirable level of inflation from inhibiting the ambitious plans of the new government. The Statement of Personal Incomes, Costs and Prices[2] presented by the Chancellor, Mr. Stafford Cripps, in February of 1948 made it clear that there was no intention to interfere with ordinary collective bargaining, though the government wished to make a case for general restraint in wage increases. This appeal for restraint succeeded in holding back the general level of wages to 5% over the next two and a half years as prices increased 8%,[3] until devaluation and the effects of the Korean War weakened adherence to the spirit of restraint.

The personal commitment to austerity demonstrated by the Chancellor may have lent a unique flavour to this period of restraint, but other features of the policy were echoed in succeeding years. The appeal to trade unions on the ground of long-term interest, the effect of leading personalities on the form and effectiveness of the policy, the acknowledgment by the unions that wage restraint might assist in building lasting prosperity - all of these characteristics came to seem hauntingly familiar.

Though the balance of payments question was more prominent than inflation in the platform of the

Conservative government elected in 1951, that ministry did make a suggestion for the control of prices and wages which was to be taken up in various forms in following years. The government floated the suggestion of a national 'advisory council,' with representation from unions and from industry, to explore methods of keeping wage increases in step with productivity. The major employers' organization expressed support for the plan, but the trade unions viewed the suggestion with some hostility, as emanating from an 'employers' government' and as a threat to the voluntary bargaining tradition.

The Conservative government were discouraged for the time being from formulating a comprehensive policy, though they did take steps indirectly, and in minor ways, to reassert their concern that inflation not get out of hand.[4] The government of Sir Anthony Eden was elected in May, 1955, in an environment of economic buoyancy. Nonetheless, there was still anxiety that prices and wages were rising too fast;[5] the Prime Minister stated on one occasion, 'We must put the battle against inflation before everything else.'[6]

The intransigence of inflation forced the Eden government - and succeeding ministries - to reconsider the view that inflation was essentially a minor by-product of post-war economic recovery and to begin to formulate a new explanation. The famous 1956 White Paper entitled The Economic Implications of Full Employment[7] did not by any means represent a repudiation of Keynesianism and all its works; the document did, however, suggest that demand management alone could not produce both price stability and full employment, and stressed the importance of productivity and industrial co-operation.

Any hopes of achieving what the White Paper termed a 'price plateau' were soon dashed by the coolness of the Trades Union Congress (TUC) to any suggestion of wage restraint, and by the new economic strains introduced by the Suez crisis. Under these conditions, the government, apparently fearing industrial conflict,[8] capitulated to wage pressure from several public sector groups, and reluctantly accepted a disappointingly high recommendation from a Court of Inquiry in the engineering industry.[9]

The government also adopted a suggestion of the Court that there should be 'an authoritative and impartial body which could give guidance as to the general principles that should govern wage

settlements.'[10]   A   Council   on   Productivity,
Prices and Incomes - nicknamed 'the Three Wise
Men' - was appointed to study general trends in
prices and incomes.   It was hoped that the Council
would have sufficient stature and independence to
lend its recommendations significant moral force.
Unfortunately, the acceptance by the Council in its
first report of what might be called a 'wage-push'
theory of inflation got it off on the wrong foot
with the unions, who virtually boycotted its work
from that time forward.[11]   The approach of the
first report, accompanied by the recommendation of a
wage freeze, gave way eventually to support for
indexed wages as the Council became less certain
that wage demands played the predominant role in
creating inflation.   The last report of this body
contained a statement tuned to the correct pitch of
despair and political consciousness to render it an
appropriate motto for British income policies for
the next eighteen years - 'at the heart of the
problem of inflation under full employment is a
state of mind.'[12]
        A renewed balance of payments problem in 1961
led the Chancellor, Mr. Selwyn Lloyd, to take more
direct action to control wages by means of a 'pay
pause.' This was to be accomplished by direct intervention in the public sector, where the government
could   exert   the   most   influence,   accompanied   by
exhortations to the private sector to make greater
efforts to hold wages in line with productivity.
The continuing hostility of the unions to anti-
inflation schemes which seemed to them disproportionately harsh on workers, as well as the absence
of   any   sign   in   the   private   sector   that   the
Chancellor's pleas for restraint were widely heeded,
doomed the 'pay pause' to failure; even in the
public sector, the policy was not pursued uniformly.
        By   1962,   the   Conservative   government   was
increasingly dissatisfied with the results of its
efforts to set the economy back on its feet through
the use of the minimally interventionist policies it
had thus far pursued.   High unemployment showed
signs of becoming endemic, Britain's stature as an
international   trading   power   seemed   to   have
diminished, and the formula for economic growth had
proved   more   elusive   than   earlier   post-war
governments had imagined.
        In February of 1962, a government White Paper,
Incomes Policy: The Next Step,[13] was published,
which evinced a new acceptance of the need for more
formal   intervention   in   the   wage   determination

process. The document suggested a 'guiding light' figure for annual wage increase of 2 - 2 1/2%, which was thought to correspond with the anticipated rise in productivity. The 'guiding light' was to be followed voluntarily, but a new body, the National Incomes Commission, was set up [14] to review particular wage settlements and to demonstrate to the parties how these settlements stood in relation to the economy as a whole. The Commission was empowered to make public reports on settlements being negotiated, with the consent of the parties in the private sector, or on a reference from the government in the public sector, and to comment retrospectively on other settlements.

The Commission did issue a small number of reports, but it suffered from several handicaps. The retrospective report was a device of limited usefulness, and lack of auxiliary staff made it impossible to conduct complete investigations of settlements in any case. The trade unions continued to withhold their approval from incomes policy, which effectively ruled out private sector cases.[15] The 'independence' of the Commission proved in reality to be isolation, as it had no way of compelling references from the government or of tracking down important cases to review, and it had no organisational connection with the other machinery of economic policy, such as the new tripartite National Economic Development Council.[16]

These weaknesses deprived the Commission of any effective persuasive power. Nonetheless, the lessons of this brief experiment were not entirely lost on subsequent policy-makers. The reference to a nationally-determined norm to be used as a guide (if never again a 'guiding light') in connection with income restraint was particularly influential in subsequent policies.

The National Economic Development Council itself, though never a central aspect of income control policies, did represent a forum - at times the only forum - where those policies, among other things, could be discussed by representatives of both sides of industry as well as of the government policy-makers and paymasters. The central place of some notion of co-ordination of economic policy among the objectives to which the Council directed itself was also an interesting clue to the increasingly Keynesian orientation of the government. It is especially interesting to note the shared assumption of the Conservative government and of the Labour government which followed in 1964

Great Britain: A Seedbed of Policy Options

that continued efforts to defeat inflation were a
concomitant of economic planning, and the essential
continuity - as to direction, at any rate - of this
aspect of policy under the two ministries. The major difference was a greater inclination on the part
of Labour to put restraint on prices and profits into the equation as well. The Labour government of
Harold Wilson arrived in office eager to find a solution to the difficulties caused by inflation. They
were also aware that direct control of incomes and
profits was not regarded with enthusiasm by either
the management or the labour side of industry.

The National Board for Prices and Incomes 1964-1970

One of the early intiatives of the new government
involved the reorganisation of those government
departments responsible for economic policy. In
theory, existing departments such as the Treasury,
the Ministry of Labour, and the Board of Trade were
to operate within a general framework of economic
planning and development created by a new
department, the Department of Economic Affairs. The
latter department's Minister and chief enthusiast,
Mr. George Brown, was commissioned to develop a
National Plan for the economy, which was to include
prices and incomes policy.

Discussions were held in late 1964 between
representatives of government, business and unions;
these resulted in a joint Statement of Intent, which
outlined the terms on which it had been agreed to
proceed.[17] In this document, the government
committed itself to 'prepare and implement a general
plan for economic development in consultation with
both sides of industry through the National Economic
Development Council.'[18] Such a general plan was
to include attention to productivity, technological
advance, manpower planning and the social assistance
system. The government was also committed to 'set
up machinery to keep a constant watch on the general
movement of prices and money incomes of all kinds',
and to use 'their fiscal powers or other appropriate
measures to correct any excessive growth in
aggregate profits as compared with the growth of
total wages and salaries.'[19]

For their part, the captains of industry and
labour swore allegiance to the following aims of
national policy:

to ensure that British industry is dynamic and
that its prices are competitive;

51

to raise productivity and efficiency so that real national output can increase, and to keep increases in wages, salaries and other forms of incomes in line with this increase;

to keep the general level of prices stable.[20]

Thus, this version of incomes policy was born in the context of a comprehensive attempt to assist economic growth; the moderation of prices and incomes was sold to business and union leaders on the basis that it would assist both constituencies in achieving their objectives of higher real incomes' and greater prosperity. A mixture of public and private enterprise, and the efforts of worker and employer would lead to greater economic benefits for all.

The Statement of Intent assigned general review of price and wage trends in the context of national economic goals to the National Economic Development Council, and stated that specific wage and price decisions would be considered by another means as yet unspecified.[21]

In the spring of 1965, the restraint machinery emerged in the form of a National Board of Prices and Incomes, which was to use as a guideline a 'norm' of 3 - 3 1/2% (again corresponding to expected increases in productivity). Again, compliance with the norm was to be voluntary, and certain exceptions were provided for; the major function of the Board was to persuade the public of the urgency and importance of conformity to the aims of the policy, and of its potential as a means of achieving the economic hopes of all sections of British society.[22]

In spite of the flexible form taken by the policy at this point, many people, especially among the unions, were not convinced by government assurances that the policy would not supplant but 'work alongside' collective bargaining, and acknowledgments that it would clearly fail if it 'removed responsibility either from ourselves or from those with whom we work in this business of negotiation.'[23] Though Mr. George Woodcock, head of the Trades Union Congress, tried to demonstrate that the term 'policy' was 'much too grandiloquent to describe what we have been about,'[24] there were others like one leader of a white-collar union, who maintained the position that British management needed to 'have upon its back the whip of high labour cost.'[25]

The Board was aware from the beginning that the consensus and self-discipline which would be required to achieve the policy's objectives would have to be carefully nurtured. Representatives of both sides of industry were included on the Board, as well as members with government and academic backgrounds, in an attempt to ensure that a variety of opinions would be heard. The Board also recruited a large staff, from the civil service and elsewhere, to assist in the study of individual cases.

Though the Board in general was seeking to secure compliance with a norm reflecting rises in productivity, the documents outlining the policy included the following four criteria for permitting deviation from the general figure:

1. where workers accepted 'more exacting work' or a major change in working practice;

2. where a pay increase would be necessary and effective in securing a desirable redistribution of labour;

3. where there was a 'general recognition' that wages or salaries were too low to maintain a 'reasonable standard of living;'

4. where there was a 'widespread recognition' that pay had fallen 'seriously out of line' with rewards for similar work elsewhere.[26]

As the Board settled into its new responsibilities, one problem which became manifest was the undesirability of being limited to commentary on a fait accompli; the government soon provided that prior notice of wage and price changes be given to the Board, with some exceptions.[27]

Price and income policy was a major issue in the 1966 election, and one member of the Board felt that it was possible for the re-elected Labour government to 'claim public approval for pursuing prices and incomes policy as much as any Government ever can.'[28] Debate over possible modification to the existing policy coincided with mounting government concern with the balance of payments and the state of the pound. It was also clear that over half of the wage settlements in the preceding fifteen months had been well above the norm.[29]

In July of 1966, the government announced that a
six-month freeze was to be imposed on prices and
incomes, followed by a six-month period of 'severe
restraint.' Over the protestations of business and
unions that voluntarism should be given a longer
trial, the government brought forward legislation to
put the dramatically new policy into effect,
legislation which, among other things, gave the
government power to enforce recommendations of the
National Board for Prices and Incomes if they were
not followed voluntarily.[30]

A freeze of the kind imposed in the summer of
1966 had the appearance of being a straightforward
and easily comprehensible mechanism, though this was
somewhat deceptive. Another White Paper[31] was
necessary explaining exactly what was to be frozen
and what was not; piecework earnings and profit-
sharing, for example, were excepted.

This turn of events was greeted with the
expected cries of outrage from trade unionists and
businessmen, but in fact government appeals to
economic exigency were fairly successful at quieting
the protest, perhaps because the freeze was seen as
a form of justice, however rough.[32] Though
critics of the policy might argue that a freeze, far
from being an effective incomes policy, was 'a
confession that you haven't got one,'[33] others
were of the opinion that the assumption by the
government of responsibility for a formal incomes
policy was an important step forward in the fight
against inflation.[34]

The period of severe restraint which commenced
at the end of January, 1967, was to be characterised
by a 'nil norm;' most wages and prices were to
continue to be frozen, though commitments made
before the freeze were to be implemented and the
Board was to be allowed to recommend increases using
its criteria concerning productivity, low pay and
manpower problems.[35]

The period was used in part as an opportunity
to consider what direction future policy should
follow. The government conceded that 'the
availability of reserve powers cannot be a
substitute for the voluntary co-operation of the
majority,'[36] and the new legislation[37]
provided that standstill powers should be replaced
by power to delay.

The residual traces of statutory regulation
contained in the new Act alarmed both the Confederation of British Industry[38] and the trade
unions.[39] The Trades Union Congress, in fact,

began to draw up plans of its own for policing
voluntary wage restraint among its affiliates, with
the hope of convincing the government that a policy
backed by statutory sanctions was unnecessary. The
government was not inspired with confidence in this
project either by what it regarded as an over-
optimistic estimate of the growth rate by the
TUC,[40] or by the meagre majority the plan
commanded at a meeting of union officials.[41]
     The government forged ahead with its own
further modifications of the policy. Any increase
in incomes would have to be justified in the light
of the four criteria - productivity, low pay,
manpower problems and gross anomalies - articulated
in earlier policy, and no increase was to be higher
than 3 1/2%.[42] The only increases to be permit-
ted above this were to be those attained by such
improvements in productivity or major reorganisation
of wage structure as to be non-inflationary.[43]
A new Prices and Incomes Act[44] extended the
powers of the government to delay wage settlements
for up to a year.
     The unions continued to grumble about the
statutory provisions which they considered inimical
to the development of consensus necessary for a
constructive anti-inflation policy. In any event,
the enhanced powers of enforcement enjoyed by the
government since 1966 did not appear to have had the
desired effect; in 1967, during the period of the
'nil' norm, earnings had risen at about 6%, and in
1968-69, were rising by about 8%.[45] The
government continued to puzzle over the conundrum of
how to obtain real compliance with its objectives
without excessively coercive measures, and in late
1969, announced its suggestion for a solution.[46]
     Though they claimed that incomes policy had
been successful in moderating the rise of incomes,
the government indicated that modest statutory
sanctions would continue for some time, in order to
prevent a burst through the limits suggested. On
the other hand, the new White Paper also emphasised
the importance over the long-run of educating the
public to an acceptance of the principle that
restraint exercised by each would lead to prosperity
for all. A 'range of norms' between 2 1/2% and
4 1/2% was to guide future administration of the
policy. This administration was to be carried out
by a new body called the Commission for Industry and
Manpower, which would consider a host of factors,
including productivity and the exigencies of the
labour market, in evaluating individual settlements;

in addition, the Commission was to examine general
and long-term issues concerning prices and incomes.

Whether this would have been a fruitful direction for development of the policy never became
clear, as the whole issue of incomes policy became
obscured by conflicts between the government and the
trade unions over proposed changes in the form of
industrial relations, and also by the excitement of
a general election which removed the Labour
government from office.

The Heath Government 1970-1974

The Conservatives under Mr. Edward Heath who had
formed the new government made clear prior to the
election their commitment to removing statutory
price and wage controls, though they had also expressed a determination to find some way of dealing
with inflation. Early requests to industry to provide information about major wage and price increases were met with considerable coolness,[47] but
the disproportion between the general level of wage
increases and that of rises in productivity inspired
anxiety. The Director-General of the National
Economic Development Council suggested that the
Council might be a vehicle for discussions about
voluntary restraint,[48] but the government was
largely preoccupied with another issue dear to its
heart - industrial relations reform.

In early 1971, however, the Chancellor
announced what came to be known as the 'n-1' policy;
the government would exert direct influence on
public sector wages, with the expectation that the
private sector would follow this example of moderation.[49] The policy did not meet these expectations. There was never much sign that the private
sector was being educated to its responsibilities.
Even in the public sector, though the government
could point to examples of wage settlements affected
by the policy, there were anomalies, notably where
the task of reaching a settlement had been confided
to a Board of Inquiry.[50] Nonetheless, the
government chose - in the face of charges that the
n-1 policy was inequitable in its fixation on public
rather than private sector workers, and on wages
rather than prices - to press on for some time. The
Prime Minister rejected suggestions of a pay freeze
as a 'return to policies which clearly and
disastrously failed in the past.'[51]

In the summer and fall of 1972, business
leaders and representatives of the unions held a
series of meetings with government officials at

which a wide range of economic issues were canvassed. These talks made some progress, even with respect to several sacred cows, and the business and labour participants, at least, seem to have felt that real negotiations were going on.

The tone of the exchange changed abruptly in early November, however, when the government made it clear that some issues were to be regarded as non-negotiable, and further announced the institution of a 90-day freeze of prices and wages.[52]

While the freeze was still in effect, further stages of the policy were announced. A Price Commission and a Pay Board were created, and a <u>Price and Pay Code</u> in the form of a statutory instrument was passed.[53] The <u>Code</u> provided, in the case of wages, for a limit of 1 pound per week per head plus 4%. This combination was intended to give extra assistance to low-paid workers as well as some flexibility in negotiation. The limit was relaxed to £ 2.25 or 7% in the third stage of the policy.[54] Orders of the Pay Board could be enforced in the courts, though the language of the empowering documents themselves was intended to be accessible to the layman. The Board used its statutory powers relatively little, and from the beginning aspired to develop a role for itself which would be more appropriate for dealing with incomes over the long term, which would enable it, for example, to deal with questions of how to deal with the anomalies which were so evident in the pay structure.[55]

Again, events conspired to prevent incomes policy from gaining any kind of equilibrium, though the epic contest between the politicians and the miners which ultimately played a large part in bringing down the government had its origins in wage demands which far exceeded the limits set in the policy.

The Social Contract 1975-78

The foundations of the policy followed by the Labour government elected in 1974 with respect to wages had been laid in discussions prior to the election between the trade unions and the Labour Party about a possible 'social contract.'[56] In return for abolition of statutory wage restraint, repeal of the <u>Industrial Relations Act</u> and changes in the tax structure, the workers would use their restored freedom to bargain moderately. The first year of the new government did not provide a good climate for such moderation, however; the international oil crisis, and other factors, led to an alarming rise in prices and wages.

The government - and the unions - accepted that some action against inflation was necessary, though statutory wage controls were considered out of the question. In July of 1975, agreement was reached on a voluntary policy, with a wage limit of Ⱡ6 per week.[57] The flat-rate form of the limit was chosen for its simplicity; it also represented a clear commitment to improvements for the low-paid, even at the expense of the traditional differentials so entrenched in the British industrial structure.[58] The workers were being asked to give a 'year for Britain,' with the burden of the sacrifice placed where it could most easily be borne.[59]

Not only was compliance with the Ⱡ6 limit virtually universal, though it was regarded more as a basic entitlement than a ceiling, but the unions were prepared to agree to a second stage policy with even more stringent limits - 5%, with a minimum increase of Ⱡ2.50 per week and a maximum of Ⱡ4.00. The vast majority of wage settlements were made in accordance with this stricter limit; there was, perhaps inevitably, greater difficulty in selling yet a third year of restraint. The unions rejected the government's suggestion of a 10% limit on earnings, though they did agree to retain a 'rule' requiring that settlements be no less than twelve months apart.[60]

The government attempted to make the 10% limit stick by other means, including the linking of government grants to the guidelines, the controversial 'blacklist' used to deny government contracts to those firms breaching the limit,[61] and government threats to use the Price Commission to reject price rises which were traceable to high pay settlements.[62]

Government attempts to secure trade union approval of a Phase Four of policy which would see a 5% limit set on earnings[63] met with little success, though talks with the Trades Union Congress produced a commitment to a 'thorough discussion' of a 'broad understanding' of inflation.[64] With the withdrawal in December of 1978 of Parliamentary approval for the withholding of government contracts as a sanction for ignoring the policy, the government embarked on a somewhat despairing search for new ways to produce compliance to its declared policy of restraint.

A New Broom: The Thatcher Government

The election of 1979 represents a turning point in the efforts of British governments to formulate and administer policies of income restraint. True, neither previous Conservative governments nor Labour governments had limited themselves rigidly to demand management policies. However firm their commitment to the logic of Keynes, governments, especially those whose faith had been shaken by the events of the 1970s, frequently supplemented demand management with monetarist experiments. It was true also that governments of both stripes, though more usually Conservative ones, had on occasion tried a laissez-faire approach.

Still, the election of the Thatcher government did signal something new, a determination to implement policies which would correspond to the tenets of newly-fashionable supply-side and monetarist theories. It is hard to describe concisely the extended policy ramifications of these theories, but there are several features of them which are of particular significance in the context of a discussion of incomes policies.

Perhaps the most serious discontinuity between previous crypto-Keynesian policies and the ideology espoused by the Thatcher government can be identified over the issue of full employment. Though policies followed prior to 1979 clearly did not produce full employment, it was generally considered to be a desirable goal. The stated commitment of the Thatcher government to liberating and nurturing the forces of the market, including the labour market, has allowed them to face mounting unemployment with equanimity. It can be explained as a short-term cost of long-term economic recovery, recovery which must be based on more efficient and productive industry. Some commentators indeed conclude that high levels of unemployment are taken by the government as evidence that the new orientation is having marked success at 'getting rid of the fat,' and putting workers on their mettle.[65]

Another change of orientation evident since 1979, again reflecting a devotion to the ideal that market forces be inhibited as little as possible, is reflected in steps taken by the Conservative government to minimise the impact of trade union activity and collective bargaining on economic activity.[66] This distinction needs perhaps to be explained a little since it is evident that previous Conservative[67] and even Labour[68] governments had made efforts to curb the power of a labour movement perceived in some quarters to be using its influence irresponsibly and in a manner inconsistent with the public interest. Indeed, all the forms of incomes policy pursued between 1945 and 1979 were perforce a challenge to the traditions of no-holds-barred or 'free' collective bargaining from which the unions, and many employers, were unwilling to deviate. Even in periods where there was no formal income restraint mechanism or no apparent policy at all, those governments made no apologies for their continued search for new ideas for mechanisms which would strike the right balance between the objective of high employment and the anxiety over inflation.[70]

This is not to deny that there were striking differences in the outlook of governments, or in the climate in which their policies were made. Generally speaking, for example, the unions showed a greater dispositon to co-operate in the initiatives taken by 'their' Labour governments on the ground that they could be trusted to follow policies useful to workers. Conservative ministries tended to view restraint of wages as a more important factor in the control of inflation than restraint of profits or prices, to see spiralling public expenditure as unacceptable, and to characterise trade unions as monopolistic and industrial conflict as intolerable. Nonetheless, during the period before 1979, there was a considerable range of shared assumptions, which included the assumption that collective bargaining was an entrenched institution which must be accommodated, if not promoted, and the assumption that government action on all fronts, fiscal and monetary, redistributive and administrative, was at least inevitable and possibly constructive.

Such assumptions lost their hold over the formation of government policy with the defeat of the Callaghan Labour government in 1979. There may be questions raised about the effectiveness of focusing on control of the money supply as the sole weapon against inflation,[71] or about whether efficiency or decimation is the likely result of Thatcherist economic policies for business,[72] or about the implications for the economy of under-mining the strength of trade unions;[73] there can, however, be little doubt of the power of the commitment of the government to monetarism and the other supply-side policies they have espoused. There also seems little doubt that the Thatcher government has had some success in bringing down the rate of inflation.

INCOMES POLICIES IN BRITISH SOCIETY

The history of British incomes policies, which has been briefly sketched here, contains numerous examples of the truism that such policies are not merely an economic affair, but have important implications in social and political terms as well. Incomes policies not only emerge in the context of particular hypotheses and assumptions about a society and about desirable objectives and values for that society, but they influence social and political development in a variety of ways. It is perhaps useful to discuss some of these implications in such summary ways as are possible in a chapter of this kind.

One of the things which makes a sensible overall evaluation of the course of British policy difficult is the change in focus from 1979. Though clearly one should not exaggerate the suddenness or thoroughness of such changes - after all, many of the same actors, who presumably share at least some common ground in their outlook on society, have been present thoughout - there is nonetheless a sense in which comparing thse two periods involves trying to bridge a fairly sizeable chasm. Though what sounds like similar language may pervade discussions of both pre- and post-1979, it is wise to keep in mind that there are clear divergences in outlook and in the assumptions on which government policies have rested.

The difficulty arises partly because supply-side economic theorists and their adherents regard it as possible to divorce economic policy more or less completely from social or political values and decisions. At the heart of their outlook lies the idea that beneficial economic results are achieved through the operation of 'natural' economic forces and the unfolding of economic 'laws;' it is trite to observe that this commits the present government to adopt policies which reduce attempts at manipulation of these forces, manipulation which, in the eyes of the supply-siders, can only be injurious to public economic welfare.[77] Thus, this government pursues what might be called 'anti-policy' in comparison with the kinds of income control mechanisms which were adopted prior to 1979. It is wise to be cautious even when one is examining periods which seem to have a lot in common, such as periods where no formal incomes policy was in place. Though the removal of formal mechanisms was at some points, notably in 1970, actuated by

61

sentiments reminiscent of those which motivate the Thatcher government, there were basic differences, the most important being the views held on collective bargaining. Previous Conservative and Labour governments aspired to curb what they saw as the excesses of unions and to bring under control the undesirable aspects of the collective bargaining system, but even in their darkest hours acknowledged the political influence of the unions and the inevitability of the endurance of collective bargaining as an institution. Collective bargaining from the viewpoint of the Thatcher government, however, is essentially an obstruction to the healthy waxing and waning of economic tides, and as such must be continually pushed and diminished.

Such differences make comparison difficult. It is nonetheless useful to focus briefly on some relevant issues which are particularly important in the British experience, and to mention some of the implications of these.

The three themes which have been particularly important in the British battle with wage inflation are the importance of productivity, the concern over the low paid and wage differentials, and the question of consensus.

Productivity and Wages
The search for the formula which would tie wages to productivity in some measurable way has from the beginning been a feature of the struggle to halt British economic decline. As noted earlier, attempts to moderate the rate of pay increases have sometimes been accompanied by the caveat that wage increases are acceptable if they are paid for out of the returns of industrial growth. Projected increases in national productivity have been frequently used to define the numerical limits which should be placed on rises in wages and prices, though such anticipated changes in productivity have rarely been achieved.

The incomes policy followed in the 1960s paid most explicit and detailed attention to the question of productivity. The policy administered by the National Board for Prices and Incomes not only attempted to see that wage limits were consistent with a global norm related to productivity, but attacked the question of productivity in relation to individual employers, industries and agreements in a way which was unique. Using its specialised staff, the Board examined the way individual companies or industries worked, and made recommendations with respect to a wide range of issues related to productivity - labour markets, the competence of management, manning practices, pay structures and so on. The Board offered, in fact, a kind of 'management consultancy' service,[75] which was regarded by some as the most promising work undertaken by that body, and which achieved a fairly wide degree of acceptance.[76]

Certainly the Chairman of the Board remained convinced that the overall productivity could not improve without conscientious efforts to increase the efficiency of individual companies, and he viewed this educational task as being of prime importance. He conceded that bringing incomes into line with productivity was a problem 'I cannot hope to solve in my lifetime;'[77] he maintained, however, that in the long term, only a similar system of specific advice given by impartial, apolitical experts could have a lasting impact on the overall level of productivity in British industry.[78]

One heavy influence on pay policy, both in the National Board for Prices and Incomes period and, to a lesser degree, in subsequent policy periods, was the phenomenon of productivity bargaining. The idea of productivity bargaining enjoyed a vogue in the mid-1960s, largely because of the miracles apparently accomplished by it in the petroleum refining industry, as described in the influential work of Allan Flanders.[79] The term 'productivity bargaining' was used to describe a form of collective bargaining in which wage increases would be explicitly traded for modifications of working practices and allocations of manpower which would serve to enhance efficiency and productivity.

The National Board for Prices and Incomes saw the concept of productivity bargaining as being very useful in the context of wage restraint: what better way to serve the aims of an inflation control programme while allowing achievements in productivity to be rewarded? The Board was thus allowed to recognise productivity agreements as an exception to the limit placed on wage agreements after 1966, provided that such agreements met the fairly rigorous standards recognized by them.[80]

The marriage of incomes policy with efforts to improve productivity brought with it some results which were not perhaps what productivity bargaining enthusiasts had hoped for. This kind of bargaining soon revealed certain limitations. It brought to light enormous difficulties of measurement[81] and gaps in understanding of the job structure.[82] It appeared to some to emphasise productivity at the expense of other legitimate considerations like safety.[83] The unions were often suspicious that it would be used primarily to reduce manning levels; employers feared that it would penalise managers who were already efficient. A major criticism was that it was difficult to conceive of productivity bargaining as a system which could continue to satisfy intitial expectations - 'tea breaks can only be sold once,' as one official put it.[84]

Needless to say, there were also suspicions that the association of productivity bargaining with relaxation of the incomes policy limits encouraged abuses. Though the National Board for Prices and Incomes cautiously concluded that productivity bargaining was not 'disadvantageous from a national point of view: rather the reverse,'[85] the feeling was widespread that productivity bargaining was being misused to make an end run around incomes policy, and that many agreements would prove in practice to have little impact on productivity. A survey in 1970 suggested that about 20% of productivity deals were spurious.[86]

When government once more excepted productivity agreements from wage limits in 1977, there was even more scepticism about the bona fides of productivity agreements, which were in some cases put together so rapidly as to preclude the kind of sober consideration and measurement which would accompany productivity bargaining in its original sense.[87]

The Thatcher government has also placed a great deal of emphasis on raised productivity as a necessary element of reducing inflation. Instead of productivity bargaining, however, the present government seeks to achieve this by allowing market forces to 'trim the fat' to streamline the economy. The government has pointed to recent information regarding the output of the British economy as signalling the success of this approach. It has been argued, however, that the figures which record the change in output, both in general terms and as a measure of individual productivity, reflect not so much a well-earned oblivion for unproductive industry, but rather a recession for all kinds of industry, productive and unproductive, and high unemployment,[88] unemployment at levels which may have surprised even the Thatcher government.[89]

The Public Sector

The productivity preoccupation of the Thatcher government is intertwined with another objective, that of reducing the size and cost of the public sector. This is in large part based on an assumption that public enterprises and public services are <u>per se</u> inefficient, though unreconstructed Keynesians argue vehemently that this view is dependent on a biased view of what is wasteful and what is not.[90] Certainly, one should not underestimate the difficulties which inhere in trying to devise sensible measures for productivity in at least those parts of the public sector which have no clear analogs in the outside world, though various ways have been suggested for approaching such a task, notably in some of the reports of the National Board for Prices and Incomes. The question is whether the objective should be to try and find ways of measuring and monitoring efficient use of public money, or whether it should be to cut back public enterprise.

In the pre-1979 period, the public sector was an obvious target for the application of incomes policies. Even without a formal effort at setting an anti-inflationary example in the public sector such as occurred with the n-1 policy in the 1950s, government commitment to limiting incomes affected the conduct of public employers. In the last few years of the Labour government, that government attempted to use the concept of cash limits on government grants to influence public sector wages and prices, rather than formal administrative mechanisms for their control. The cash limit appproach has also, of course, been used by the Thatcher government in its attempts to restrain public spending. The adoption of cash limits, with or without a monetarist explanation for that adoption, suggests that anxiety about the relationship between recession, inflation and growth in the public sector, is a well-entrenched feature of recent times.

It is difficult to draw any hard and fast conclusions about the role of the public sector in promoting inflation. There is considerable debate about whether current evidence is consistent with the assumption that large-scale government spending is inherently inflationary; the evidence seems, at best, equivocal.[91]

The association of public sector wages, and public sector spending in general, with the question of inflation, presents more clearly than any other issue the dilemma faced by British governments.

Whether the squeezing of the public sector represents, as it did for some years before 1979, an
attempt to bring Keynesian public spending under
greater control, or whether it rests, as it does in
the Thatcher period, on a more fundamental antag-
onism to the welfare state, it seems to stem from an
awareness of the difficulties of balancing welfare
objectives with the health of the economy as a
whole. The insistence of the Thatcher government
that the social costs of reducing the public sector
share of the economy are, at least in the short run,
an irrelevant consideration, flies in the face of
earlier assumptions that the social implications
must be put in the balance against the objectives of
any economic policy. Whatever criticisms may be
made of the success of the British welfare state
before 1979 in attaining its social objectives, it
is surely dangerous to draw the conclusion that
social objectives should be left entirely out of
account when assessing economic policy. Supply-side
economists would perhaps argue that this dichotomy
is misleading, that social objectives will ultimately be met in the new economic order, yet it is hard
to maintain faith in this proposition when supply-
side policy seems so prodigal with human costs.[92]

Incomes Policy and Social Justice
The second theme which has been of enormous importance in the unfolding of British policies concerning incomes has to do with what might loosely be
termed questions of justice. These issues have mani-
fested themselves in every period of incomes policy,
in the formation and administration of policy, and
in the public discussion of and reaction to policy.

There are several major issues which arise in
this context, the first of them concerning the fate
of low-paid workers in any period of restraint.
Concern that low-paid workers are going to suffer
disproportionately when their already meagre wages
are further restrained led in periods when formal
pay policy was in effect to the presentation of
arguments that the low-paid should be protected from
the full force of income limits. Except for those
short periods when a freeze was in effect, periods
of statutory incomes policy made allowances for low
pay.

The National Board for Prices and Incomes
scheme specifically excepted low pay from the limits
applied to wages. After wrestling on several
occasions with the problem of deciding what

constituted low pay in particular cases, the Board engaged in a more general examination of the problems of low pay.[93] Though the Board did not deny that low pay was a problem, or that a restraint programme should take cognisance of it, they found it difficult to fix on any working definition or measure of low pay, and concluded that low pay was often closely linked to other problems such as industrial inefficiency or decline in customer demand.

The policy administered by the Pay Board in 1973 and 1974 attempted to deal with low pay in a slightly different fashion, through the application of norms which combined a percentage limit with minimum increases which were intended to have a relatively less serious impact on the low-paid.

The first phase of the Social Contract also articulated wage limits in the form of a flat rate, which was consistent with the ideas of social responsibility and self-sacrifice which the unions put forward as the motivation for accepting restraint.[94]

There has been considerable skepticism about the overall effect of incomes policies on the position of those earning low wages, with many subscribing to the wary sentiments expressed by the leader of a group of low-paid workers that any temporary cessation of demands by higher-paid workers would be followed by a 'mad rush to make up for what they had lost.'[95]

The stance of the policies of the Thatcher government towards the low-paid is that artificial assistance to the low-paid is merely another obstacle to labour market forces which will improve their lot in the long run by strengthening the economy as a whole. The recent abolition of Wages Councils, the mechanism in place to establish wage floors in certain industries where there was no collective bargaining, is an illustration of this theory in action.

Certainly the evidence of earlier periods of anti-inflation policy, when attempts were made to mitigate the harshness of restraint on low-paid workers, gives little support to the proposition that incomes policies can secure any significant long-term redistribution of wage scales in favour of the low-paid.[96] This is partly because low wages - as distinct from poverty - are difficult to treat as a social problem; there are so many contributing factors, such as industrial inefficiency, low skill levels, stagnant markets, undesirable jobs and so on, that it is difficult to generalise about low pay or to treat it in isolation.

Furthermore, such concern as government, employers and unions might display for the low-paid was counterbalanced by a commitment equally strong, perhaps stronger, to the maintenance of differentials between various categories of workers. There is perhaps no country where the industrial 'league table' of differentials is regarded as so authoritative. Differentials, at least those based on skill, are clearly a feature of Labour and Conservative labour market theory, and the maintenance of the differential pattern is viewed by many as essential to any wage policy which is going to appear just. Though there may be differences between those Keynesians who think wage differentials are amenable to a scientific job classification system and those neo-conservatives who think differentials better left to the market, the discussion is not really over whether differentials should be preserved, but over how they should be maintained.

Whether a wage policy is viewed as just or fair in terms of the similarity of the treatment it accords to everyone, or in terms of the maintenance of a wage pattern, it is likely that it will eventually come to be viewed as unfair. There seems an inherent instability in such policies, a product of anomalies which have been preserved and perpetuated, like bubbles within the policy, or of the failure of the set of rules which govern wage increases to adapt to changing circumstances.

Incomes Policy and Consensus

The perception that a policy is fair or just is important because of the dependence of such policies for their success on a consensus for their acceptance among those affected by them. The importance of public consensus is, of course, well-known to those who seek to introduce policy or regulation of any kind, and consensus-building has been one of the great preoccupations of modern regimes.

The pattern of British policy up to 1979 offers several examples of the collapse of consensus and the subsequent fading away of incomes policy. It has been suggested that no incomes policy can cope with 'union market power by way of consent' and that they are all doomed to founder eventually 'on the rock of relativities and differentials.'[97]

It is perhaps less surprising that consensus became unstable and collapsed in the face of compounding anomalies, and impatience with those distortions of wage patterns which were bound to occur, than that the consensus could, apparently, be reconstructed again so often; that a population who had been assured with regularity since the war that if they consented to restraint one more time, if they accepted a new form of wage limit, if they put up with the National Board for Prices and Incomes (or Pay Board or Social Contract), the battle with inflation would be won this time and economic recovery would move forward, would participate so readily in yet another pay policy initiative. Consensus might reflect acquiescence rather than approval, consensus might not stretch beyond the vaguest understanding of the policy, but there was generally a surprising willingness to give the new policy a chance.

At the same time, of course, this consensus was inherently fragile, and could not survive the disappointments and apparent injustices which were dealt out as these policies unfolded. It would be hard for the supporters of any policy to claim that they had unlocked the secret of making incomes policy acceptable in the long term. The graduates of the National Board for Prices and Incomes remained convinced that the kind of approach they followed was the most promising,[98] though it would achieve results only slowly, but they did not claim to have hit upon a balance between the coercive and the voluntary which could maintain consensus indefinitely.

It might be argued that the Thatcher government has abondoned the search for consensus, or perhaps regards consensus as irrelevant. It is doubtful that they would see it in these terms, but a view which sees the economy as essentially amenable only to natural forces, and not to conscious manipulation, is bound to place less emphasis on the necessity for consent in the administration of economic policy.

CONCLUSION

It is beyond the scope of this chapter to draw any conclusions about the correctness of neo-conservative theory in economic terms. From the point of view of supply-side orthodoxy, the logic of the unfolding of natural economic forces demands that the cries of social and political critics, the calls for social action and reference to political consensus, be treated as of little account. It is this acceptance of the isolation of economic issues from social and political ones which makes it impossible to assess the policies of the present government on the same terms as those of previous regimes.

It has been argued[99] that during the period before 1979, changes in the British class structure made it more difficult to build consensus, and that this, in fact, may have contributed to inflationary pressures. If this is correct, it means that efforts to control inflation which have a consensual basis would become ever more difficult.

Somehow the answer to this does not seem to be to abandon the search, or to characterise social adhesion behind government policy as irrelevant. If social characteristics, political opinions and the other untidy features of British society are in the end of no consequence to the course of economic events, as supply-side theorists argue, economic theories and economic policies still unquestionably have an impact on social and political development. The danger of ignoring this is that, even if economic policy is successful in its own terms, the costs for society are too high.

FOOTNOTES

1. Partly as a result of the global oil crisis.
2. (Cmnd. 7321), 1948.
3. Dow, J.C.R., The Management of the British Economy (Cambridge University Press, Cambridge, 1964), p. 35.
4. Fels, Allen, The Prices and Incomes Board (Cambridge University Press, Cambridge, 1972), p. 7. For example, the remission of several decisions of Wages Councils for reconsideration.
5. Knowles, K.G.J.C., 'Wages and Productivity,' in G.D.N. Worswick and P.H. Ady (ed.) The British Economy in the 1950s (Oxford University Press, Oxford, 1962) p. 503.
6. Fisher, Nigel, Iain Macleod (Andre Deutsch, London, 1973), p. 107.
7. (Cmnd. 9725), March, 1956.
8. Knowles, 'Wages', p. 508.
9. Fisher, Iain Macleod, p. 119.

Great Britain: A Seedbed of Policy Options

10. Quoted in Guillebaud, G.W., _Wage Determination and Wage Policy_ (James Nisbet & Co., Welwyn, 1967), p. 38.
11. Fels, _The Prices and Incomes Board_, p. 10.
12. Quoted in Knowles, 'Wages', p. 515.
13. (Cmnd. 1626), February, 1962.
14. _The National Incomes Commission_ (Cmnd. 1844), November, 1962.
15. Guillebaud, _Wage Determination_, p. 42.
16. Fels, _The Prices and Incomes Board_, p. 16.
17. _Joint Statement of Intent on Productivity, Prices and Incomes_ (HMSO, 1964), para. 5.
18. Ibid., para. 6.
19. Ibid., para. 8.
20. Ibid., para. 9.
21. Ibid., para. 10.
22. Mitchell, Joan, _The National Board for Prices and Incomes_ (Secker and Warburg, London, 1971), p. 8.
23. TUC. 'Productivity, Prices and Incomes: Report of a Conference of Executive Committees of Affiliated Organizations,' p. 27.
24. Ibid., p. 33.
25. Ibid., p. 48.
26. _Prices and Incomes Policy_ (Cmnd. 2639), April, 1965.
27. _Prices and Incomes Policy: An Early-Warning System_ (Cmnd. 2808), November, 1965.
28. Mitchell, _The National Board_, p. 12.
29. Incomes Data Services, _Panorama April 1965 - July 1966_, quoted in Balfour, Campbell, _Incomes Policy and the Public Sector_ (Routledge and Kegan Paul, London, 1972), p. 16.
30. _Prices and Incomes Act 1966_, 1966, c. 33
31. _Prices and Incomes Standstill_ (Cmnd. 3073), July, 1966.
32. Mitchell, _The National Board_, p. 14.
33. Cairncross, Sir Alec, in _On Incomes Policy: Papers and Proceedings in Honour of Erik Lundberg_ (Industrial Council for Economic Research, Stockholm, 1969), p. 39.
34. Drake, Charles D. 'The Prices and Incomes Act in its Wider Setting,' _Journal of Business Law_ (1967), p. 17.
35. _Prices and Incomes Standstill: The Period of Severe Restraint_ (Cmnd. 3150), November, 1966.
36. _Prices and Incomes Policy after 30 June, 1967_ (Cmnd. 3255), March, 1967.
37. _Prices and Incomes Act 1967_, 1967, c. 53.
38. 'Freeze Shock for CBI,' _Times_, 7 February, 1967.

71

39. 'Union Warning on Law to Curb Pay,' Times, 23 February, 1967.
40. Thomas, Michael, 'TUC Told to Think Again on Wages,' Times, 19 December, 1967.
41. 'Harder Line on Pay Seems Certain,' Times, 29 February, 1968.
42. Prices, Productivity and Incomes in 1968 and 1969 (Cmnd. 3590), April, 1968.
43. Ibid., para. 34.
44. Prices and Incomes Act 1968, 1968, c. 42.
45. Clegg, Hugh, How to Run an Incomes Policy And Why We Made Such A Mess of the Last One (Heinemann, London, 1971), p. 13.
46. Productivity, Prices and Incomes after 1969, (Cmnd. 4237), December, 1969,
47. 'Incomes Policy or Not?' Financial Times, 1 October, 1980.
48. Corina, Maurice, 'Call for Voluntary Pay Controls,' Financial Times, 17 November, 1970.
49. Brittan, Samuel, 'Inflation: Barber Looks to Pay Policy,; Financial Times, 20 January, 1971.
50. Balfour, Income Policy, p. 161.
51. Evans, Richard, 'Heath Rejects Freeze on Wages and Prices.' Financial Times, 15 June, 1972.
52. A Programme for Controlling Inflation: The First Stage (Cmnd. 5125), November, 1972, Counter-Inflation (Temporary Provisions) Act 1972, 1972, c. 74.
53. The Programme for Controlling Inflation: The Second Stage (Cmnd. 5205), January, 1973; The Counter-Inflation Programme: The Operation of Stage Two (cmnd. 5267), March, 1973; Counter-Inflation Act 1973, 1973, c. 9; The Counter-Inflation (Price and Pay Code) Order 1973, 1973, No. 658.
54. The Price and Pay Code for Stage Three: A Consultative Document (Cmnd. 5444), October, 1973.
55. Pay Board, 'Experience of Operating a Statutory Incomes Policy,' (1974) para. 88, p. 30.
56. TUC. 'Collective Bargaining and the Social Contract,' 26 June, 1974, p. 4.
57. The Attack on Inflation (Cmnd. 6151), July, 1975; TUC, 'The Development of the Social Contract,' July, 1975.
58. Ibid.
59. Wyles, John, 'Jones Calls on Union to Fight Inflation,' Financial Times, 25 July, 1975.
60. TUC, 109th Annual Congress Report, September, 1977, Composite Motion No. 7 on 'Wages and Economic Policy.'
61. Holliday Hall v. Chapple and Other, Times, 7 February, 1978,

62. Labour Research Department, 'Guide to Pay Bargaining, 1977-78,' p. 13.

63. Winning the Battle Against Inflation (Cmnd. 7293), July, 1978.

64. Into the '80's: An Agreement; See Paul Routledge, 'Cabinet-TUC Accord on Annual Pay Talks,' Times, 23 July, 1978.

65. See e.g. Hodgson, Geoff, 'Thatcherism: The Miracle That Never Happened' in Nell, Edward (ed.) Free Market Conservatism: A Critique of Theory and Practice (George Allen & Unwin, London, 1984), p. 185 ('The New Right is attached to the Victorian doctrine that all good medicine is painful medicine, and if it does not cause pain, then it cannot be doing any good.'), and p. 202.

66. Employment Act, 1980, 1980, c. 42; Employment Act, 1982, c. 46.

67. E.g. Industrial Relations Act, 1971, c. 72.

68. E.g. In Place of Strife: A Policy for Industrial Relations (Cmnd. 3888), January, 1969.

69. For an interesting discussion on this point, see the 'Introduction' by Paul Davies and Mark Freedland to their Third Edition of Kahn-Freund's Labour and the Law (Stevens, London, 1983).

70. Ibid. p. 7.

71. See Kaldor, N., 'Monetarism and U.K. Monetary Policy,' Cambridge Journal of Economics vol. 4 (December, 1980).

72. Tomlinson, J., 'Does Mass Unemployment Matter?' (February, 1983) National Westminster Bank Quarterly Review.

73. Hodgson, 'Thatcherism,' p. 198.

74. Jackson, Dudley, H.A. Turner et al, Do Trade Unions Cause Inflation? (Cambridge University Press, Cambridge, 1972), p. 62.

75. Interview with Mr. R. Hodgson (British Printing Corporation), 1978.

76. See Bilson, R.E., The Effect of Incomes Policy on Collective Bargaining in Great Britain and Canada, 1964-1978, (unpublished dissertation, London, 1982), Chapters 2 and 3.

77. Cairncross, Frances, 'Control of Incomes the Big Problem - Jones,' Times, 3 April, 1978,

78. Interview with Mr. Aubrey Jones (NBPI), 1978.

79. Flanders, Allan, The Fawley Productivity Agreements (Faber and Faber, London, 1964). See also E. Owen Smith, Productivity Bargaining (Pan Books, London, 1971).

80. NBPI, Reports No. 231 and 316.

Productivity Bargaining, and see Aubrey Jones, The New Inflation: The Politics of Prices and Incomes (Andre Deutsch, London, 1973), pp. 81-90.
81. Interview with Sir Henry Phelps Brown, 1978.
82. Interview with Mr. Aubrey Jones (NBPI), 1978.
83. TUC, Productivity Bargaining. p. 31.
84. Interview with Mr. L. Ambrose (AUEW and CAC), 1978.
85. NBPI, Report No. 123, Productivity Agreements (Cmnd. 4136).
86. Evans, E.W., 'The Rise and Fall of Productivity Bargaining,' (Autumn 1972) Moorgate and Wall Street, p. 69.
87. Interview with Mr. David Cockroft and Mr. Colin Cummings (TUC).
88. Hodgson, 'Thatcherism,' p. 194.
89. Stewart, Michael, Controlling the Economic Future: Policy Dilemmas in a Shrinking World (Wheatsheat Books, Brighton, 1983), p. 82.
90. Heilbroner, Robert, 'Capitalism as Gestalt - A Contrast of Visions,' in Edward T. Nell (ed.) Free Market Conservatism, p. 7.
91. See Kaldor, 'Monetarism'; Hodgson, 'Thatcherism'; Peacock, Alan T. and Martin Ricketts, 'The Growth of the Public Sector and Inflation' in Hirsch, Fred and John Goldthorpe (eds.) The Political Economy of Inflation (Martin Robertson, London, 1978), Chapter 5.
92. Heilboner, 'Capitalism,' p. 9.
93. NBP, Report No. 169, General Problems of Low Pay (Cmnd. 4648) April, 1971.
94. Interview with Sir Henry Phelps Brown, 1978.
95. Lord Allen of USDAW, in TUC, 'Economic Policy and Collective Bargaining in 1973,' p. 77.
96. Bilson, op. cit., p. 212-214.
97. Brittan, Samuel, 'Inflation and Democracy,' in Hirsch and Goldthorpe, Political Economy, p. 176.
98. Mitchell, The National Board, and Jones, The New Inflation.
99. Goldthorpe, John H., 'The Current Inflation: Towards a Sociological Account,' in Hirsch and Goldthorpe (eds.), Political Economy, p. 196.

REFERENCES

The Attack on Inflation (Cmnd. 6151), July, 1975.

Balfour, Campbell, Income Policy and the Public Sector (Routledge and Kegan Paul, London, 1972).

Bilson, R.E., The Effect of Incomes Policy on Collective Bargaining in Great Britain and Canada, 1964-1978, unpublished dissertation, University of London, 1982.

Brittan, Samuel, The Role and Limits of Government: Essays in Political Economy, (Temple Smith, London, 1984).

Cairncross, Sir Alec, in On Incomes Policy: Papers and Proceedings in Honour of Erik Lundberg (Industrial Council for Economic Research, Stockholm, 1969).

Clegg, Hugh, How to Run an Incomes Policy and Why We Made Such A Mess of the Last One, (Heinemann, London, 1971).

Counter-Inflation Act, 1973, 1973, c.9.

The Counter-Inflation Programme: The Operation of Stage Two (Cmnd. 5267), March, 1973.

The Counter-Inflation (Price and Pay Code) Order 1973, 1973, No. 658.

Counter-Inflation (Temporary Provisions) Act, 1972, 1972. c. 74.

Davies, Paul and Mark Freedland (eds.), Kahn-Freund's Labour and the Law (Stevens, London, 1983).

Dow, J.C.R., The Management of the British Economy (Cambridge University Press, Cambridge, 1964).

Drake, Charles D., 'The Prices and Incomes Act in its Wider Setting,' Journal of Business Law (1967).

The Economic Implications of Full Employment (Cmnd. 9725), March, 1956.

Fels, Allen, The Prices and Incomes Board (Cambridge University Press, Cambridge, 1972).

Fishbein, Warren H., Wage Restraint by Consensus: Search for an Incomes Policy Agreement, 1965-79 (Routledge & Keegan Paul, London, 1984).

Fisher, Nigel, Iain Macleod (Andre Deutsch, London, 1973).

Flanders, Allan, The Fawley Productivity Agreements (Faber andd Faber, London, 1964).

Guillebaud, G.W., Wage Determination and Wage Policy (James Nisbet & Co., Welwyn, 1967).

Hirsch, Fred and John Goldthorpe (eds), The Political Economy of Inflation (Martin Robertson, London, 1978).

In Place of Strife: A Policy for Industrial Relations (Cmnd. 3888), January, 1969.

Incomes Data Services, Panorama April 1965 - July 1966.

Industrial Relations Act, 1971, 1971, c. 72.

Jackson, Dudley, K.A. Turner et al (eds.) Do Trade Unions Cause Inflation? (Cambridge University Press, Cambridge, 1972).

Joint Statement of Intent on Productivity, Prices, and Incomes (HMSO, 1964).

Jones, Aubrey, The New Inflation: The Politics of Prices and Incomes (Andre Deutsch, London, 1973).

Kaldor, N. 'Monetarism and U.K. Monetary Policy,' Cambridge Journal of Economics, Vol. 4 (December, 1980).

Mitchell, Joan, The National Board for Prices and Incomes (Secker and Warburg, London, 1971).

National Board for Prices and Incomes, General Problems of Low Pay, (Cmnd. 4648), April, 1971, Productivity Bargaining, Reports No. 231 and 316.

The National Incomes Commission, (Cmnd. 1844), November, 1962.

Nell, Edward (ed.), Free Market conservatism: A Critique of Theory and Practice (George Allen & Unwin, London, 1984).

Pay Board, 'Experience of Operating a Statutory Incomes Policy' (1974).

Prices and Incomes Act, 1966, 1966, c. 33.

Prices and Incomes Act, 1967, 1967, c. 53.

The Price and Pay Code for Stage Three: A Consultative Document (Cmnd. 8444), October, 1973.

Prices and Incomes Act, 1968, 1968, c. 42.

Prices and Incomes Policy (Cmnd. 2639), April, 1965.

Prices and Incomes Policy After 30 June, 1967 (Cmnd. 3255), March, 1967.

Prices and Incomes Policy: An Early-Warning System (Cmnd. 2808), November, 1965.

Prices and Incomes Standstill (Cmnd. 3073), July, 1966.

Prices and Incomes Standstill: The Period of Severe Restraint (Cmnd. 3150), November, 1966.

Prices, Productivity and Incomes in 1968 and 1969 (Cmnd. 3590), April, 1968.

Productivity, Prices and Incomes after 1969 (Cmnd. 4237), December, 1969.

A Programme for Controlling Inflation: The First Stage (Cmnd. 5125), November, 1973.

The Programme for Controlling Inflation: The Second Stage (Cmnd. 5205), January, 1973.

Smith, E. Owen, Productivity Bargaining (Pan Books, London, 1978).

Statement on Personal Incomes, Costs and Prices (Cmnd. 7321), 1948.

Stewart, Michael, Controlling the Economic Future: Policy Dilemmas in a Shrinking World (Wheatsheaf Books, Brighton, 1983).

Tomlinson, J., 'Does Mass Unemployment Matter?' National

Westminster Bank Quarterly Review, (February, 1983).

Trades Union Congress, 109th Annual Congress Report, September, 1977.

Trades Union Congress, 'Collective Bargaining and the Social Contract,' 26 June, 1974.

Trades Union Congress, The Development of the Social Contract, July, 1975.

Trades Union Congress, Productivity Bargaining.

Trades Union Congress, 'Productivity, Prices and Incomes: Report of a Conference of Executive Committees of Affiliated Organizations' (April, 1965).

Winning the Battle Against Inflation (Cmnd. 7293), July, 1980.

Worswick, G.D.N. and P.H. Ady (eds.), The British Economy in the 1950s (Oxford University Press, Oxford, 1962).

Chapter Three

AUSTRALIA: NEW WINE INTO OLD BOTTLES

Malcolm Rimmer

INTRODUCTION

Incomes policies have become the subject of intense
controversy in Australia. Partly this is because
economists disagree. On the one hand there are
those who consider incomes policies an indispensable
tool for macroeconomic management. They regard
centralised control of pay as the best way to reduce
inflation and unemployment and to ensure steady
economic growth.[1]
     Their critics condemn such a system. It is,
they say, incompatible with the efficient
microeconomic functioning of the labour market,
preventing wage flexibility from allocating labour
and clearing the labour market. The results,
ultimately, can only be higher unemployment and
inflation and lower economic growth.[2]
Deregulation is their solution to labour market
problems. How is this to be done? This depends
upon what kind of industrial relations institutions
best suit a particular labour market policy.
     As the recent Hancock Committee of Review has
illustrated, two options are widely identified.[3]
Supporters of incomes policy endorse a continuing
strong role for Australia's compulsory arbitration
tribunals which have become a de facto incomes
policy administration. The opponents of incomes
policy would like to dismantle or weaken that system
adopting in its place a collective bargaining system
which may allow more wage flexibility and so be more
compatible with a deregulated labour market.[4]
     Politicians have not been reluctant to seize
upon these differences of opinion. Since 1983, the
traditional bi-partisan support for compulsory
arbitration has faded and a gap has opened between
party policies. The Australian Labour party remains

strongly attached to a corporatist solution to labour market problems, using a centralised arbitration system to extract business and labour support for an incomes policy.[5] Australia's conservative parties, the Liberal/National parties, increasingly lean to an opposing view. Extreme economic liberalism has a grip upon the 'dry' right wing of the coalition. Since April 1984, when the Liberal party adopted a compromise policy upon industrial relations, the influence of the right has grown to the point that a future conservative government would seem unlikely to continue with incomes policy.

Whether a deregulated labour market could be established, and whether it would work better than a centralised incomes policy are questions for the future if at all. Australia has no real experience upon which to make an assessment. In contrast, an assessment of incomes policy is possible, since various forms of incomes policy have been applied throughout the past ten years.

Table 1 below shows the main phases of incomes policy in the decade 1975-1985. Of these, the first - wage indexation - was the most significant, maintaining strong centralised control over pay for six years. To call the second of these phases - the 'case-by-case' system - an incomes policy may be a misnomer since it was a weak, decentralised system - a 'thaw' after six years of strict regimentation under the wage indexation system that preceded it. Nevertheless, we will classify it as a phase of incomes policy, since attempts were made to 'standardise' wage movements in this period. It ended abruptly in December 1982 when the wage freeze was imposed. In September 1983, shortly after the freeze ended, a new incomes policy was introduced - the Prices and Incomes Accord - which is in operation at the time of writing. The 'Accord' is, in many ways, identical to the old wage indexation system that proved so durable between 1975 and 1981.

These four phases of policy can be divided into two types. First are the long-term, equity-based, income growth policies. Wage indexation and the Accord illustrate this kind of approach. Second are short-term, economic adjustment policies. Both the case-by-case system and the wage freeze illustrate this kind of policy. The most important of the two types, measured by duration of operation, is the first. Of the past ten years, eight have been spent under long-term policies.

Table 1 - Phases of Incomes Policy: 1975-1985

Policy	Period of Application	Major Wage-Fixing Criteria	Degree of Central Control
1. Wage Indexation	April 1975 to July 1981	(a) Pay linked to Prices and Productivity (b) Most other forms of increase prohibited	HIGH
2. Case-by-Case System	August 1981 to December 1982	No explicit criteria	LOW
3. Wage-Freeze	December 1982 to September 1983	Virtually no wage increases permitted	VERY HIGH
4. Prices and Incomes Accord	September 1983 to present	(a) Pay linked to Prices & Productivity (b) Most other forms of increase prohibited.	HIGH

The defining characteristics of the first type of policy establishing them as 'equity-based' policies, are the criteria for income growth. Equity, for our purposes, has two dimensions. The first concerns the establishment of a fair general level of wages. The second has to do with fair relative pay between groups of workers. The solution to the first question has been to adjust pay to compensate for changes in the cost of living and in productivity. This maintains the real value of wages and allows workers to share in the growing wealth of the economy. The answer to the second question is more difficult. Generally since 1975 incomes policies have assumed wage relativities to be fair unless unions can demonstrate that the 'work value' of a particular group has changed.[6] Excepting adjustments of this kind, fairness is preserved by awarding strictly uniform wage increases to the whole workforce.

An incomes policy that secures 'equity' by

giving full wage indexation and productivity increases to workers is not a wage restraint policy except under extreme conditions of union bargaining strength. Wage restraint in Australia is possible because the prices and productivity criteria have not been applied automatically. Instead the size of increase to be granted under both criteria is open to debate. Under adverse economic conditions, discounting can take place.

This leads to the second defining feature of these policies, the procedure by which this discretionary adjustment process occurs. Of special importance here are the periodic semi-judicial public hearings, known as national wage cases, where debate occurs over the amount of consumer price or productivity increase that will be handed on to workers' wage packets. In these hearings a panel (Full Bench) of the Australian Conciliation and Arbitration Commission (the Commission) hears and adjudicates upon submissions from the main interested parties - the federal and state governments, the Australian Council of Trade Unions (ACTU) and the Confederation of Australian Industry (CAI).

The short-term policies of the last ten years are more varied in form than these equity-based schemes and resemble each other only in that they are prompted by extreme economic pressures. For example, a very uneven resources boom in 1980-1 created demands for a less uniform approach to wage determination - demands that were met by the case-by-case system. Second, the freeze arose out of a particularly severe economic recession in 1982-3. The rationale for both policies ended with the easing of the economic circumstances that had brought them into existence.

Australia's experience of incomes policies therefore has been both prolonged and distinctive. Particularly unusual has been the strong emphasis formally given to equity criteria in framing such incomes policies. Against this, however, economic flexibility has been available both through the wage restraint decisions made in a number of national wage cases and in such dramatic shifts of policy as those that occurred in 1981 and 1982-3.

THE INDUSTRIAL, ECONOMIC AND LEGAL ENVIRONMENT

That equity-based incomes policies should work for as long as they have is remarkable, for the

81

Australian environment is by no means perfectly suited to this approach to wage determination. There are three special areas of difficulty.

First is the nature of trade union power which tends to destabilise equity-based incomes policies. Since 1974 unionised labour has accounted for over 55% of the workforce.[7] As a result unions, as collectively represented by the ACTU, possess considerable strength. This strength has been recognised by governments which have chosen to negotiate incomes policies with the ACTU. For example, wage indexation was negotiated between the ACTU and the government in 1974-5[8] and the Accord arose quite clearly from union-Labour party bargaining in 1982-3.[9] The importance of equity criteria in successive incomes policies can be explained largely by the influence of trade union centres over these negotiations.

Since the ACTU represents unions generally it has sought wages principles which maintain uniformity between different groups of unionised workers. This matches poorly the real distribution of power within the union movement. Some unions, particularly in declining manufacturing industries, are very weak. Others, in transport, oil, minerals and power, for example, are very strong. Powerful unions are often reluctant to concede that wages should be settled by reference to anything other than their own bargaining strength. Paradoxically then, an equity-based incomes policy can be upset by divisions within the union movement which has used its general strength to secure such a policy in the first place. The problem facing the ACTU is to find a way to control its stronger members in the interests of the weaker ones.

The second problem concerns the nature of the Australian economy which again is likely to upset an equity-based policy. A small dependent economy with a large trading sector - exports and imports, for example, run at around 15% of GDP - it is heavily influenced by world trends in investment, interest rates and export commodity prices. As a result, governments find that their hands are tied in key areas of economic policy and they have to place heavy reliance upon a narrow range of domestic policy variables. Wages and taxation are amongst the most important of these. Since the oil crisis in 1974 a persistent adverse world economic environment has existed, increasing the likelihood of excessive recourse to wage restraint. Indeed, governments have tried to use wage restraint almost continuously - against the spirit of the equity criteria in incomes policies.

This problem is exacerbated by the volatility of the Australian economy induced by heavy dependence upon commodity exports which are sold upon notoriously unstable world markets. Such instability has a corrosive effect upon the capacity of the economy to maintain stable real wages. Furthermore there is a high degree of sectoral inequality in the impact of these fluctuations upon industry profitability and therefore union bargaining power. These variations, if not moderated by exchange rate policy, undermine the capacity of the economy to sustain wage uniformity. In particular, pressure for a wage breakout can occur in an overheated export sector of the economy.[10]

As a result of these characteristics of the economy, incomes policies occupy an uncomfortable place in the mixture of government macroeconomic policy devices. There is a perverse consequence to this. Incomes policies normally require support from complementary fiscal, monetary and exchange rate policies.[11] Such is the nature of the Australian economy that the opposite commonly occurs, and incomes policy is used to compensate for deficient government control in other branches of macroeconomic policy. The weakness of government economic policy and the volatile nature of the economy make it difficult to sustain the economic conditions to support an equity-based incomes policy for long.

The third area of difficulty is a political-legal one. This problem complicates the task of negotiating an incomes policy. First, the federal government has no constitutional power to control wages directly. The state governments can do this but they have little responsibility for economic management and so exercise their power usually at the request of the Commonwealth. Incomes policies must then be negotiated between the federal and the state governments.

Yet this is not the only or even the most important way the federal government can act. It does have the power under Section 51 (xxxv) of the Federal Constitution to legislate:

> With respect to conciliation and arbitration for the prevention and settlement of industrial disputes extending beyond the limits of one State.

In practice this has come to mean it can
establish a semi-judicial tribunal, the Australian
Conciliation and Arbitration Commission, which can
fix pay directly at least for part of the workforce.
Here again the government only has influence rather
than direct power. It can operate an incomes policy
through the Arbitration Commission but first must
persuade this body of the need to do so.

In a democratic political system incomes
policies must normally be negotiated between the
interested parties. In Australia such negotiations
are unusually complicated because of the number of
parties to them, including unions, employers,
federal and state governments and independent tribunals. Intruding into such negotiations, there is
likely also to be a conflict between unions who
generally seek to base wages upon equity and employers who care more about the state of the
economy. In such a context, securing consent to run
an incomes policy reflects either a temporary coincidence of interests or a triumph of political will
and negotiating skill.

GOVERNMENT, INDUSTRIAL TRIBUNALS AND INCOMES POLICY

Credit for the establishment of incomes policies
since 1975 lies largely with federal governments who
have seen the need for such policies and been persuasive advocates for them. However, credit for
their successful operation should more properly be
given to the arbitration tribunals.

Australia's arbitration tribunals have the task
of fixing award rates of pay. The most important
tribunal, the Australian Conciliation and Arbitration Commission, was established in 1905, and in
1983 made awards covering 34.7% of the workforce.
The six state tribunals cover more workers - 50.7%
of the workforce in 1983 - but for historical and
practical reasons now follow the leadership of the
federal Commission over pay.[12]

Phelps Brown has remarked on the fortunate
accident by which Australia found in such tribunals
a ready-made incomes policy administration.[13]
It was not, however, a suitable machinery to begin
with. Taking to the task in the 1940s, the
tribunals took several decades to learn the skills
of running an incomes policy. Moreover, they still
approach the task in an unusual way. Three pecu-
liarities stand out.

First, the primary statutory duty of tribunals

is still to resolve industrial disputes; consequently they must remain more sensitive to industrial relations issues than an incomes policy administration charged only with inflation control.
Second, they are long-standing bodies outliving what
seem inevitably to be temporary phases of incomes
policy. This gives them an unrivalled degree of
political independence as well as a core of experience that their ephemeral overseas counterparts
often lack. Third, since most tribunals originated
as courts, they are still staffed partly by personnel with a legal background and are governed by
constitutional, statute and case law; they are
unavoidably more legalistic than their equivalents
in other countries.

Given their unusual organisational character,
how do these tribunals go about the task of running
an incomes policy? The central task of incomes
policy administration may be defined as gaining
consent from powerful labour market institutions for
general rules about wage determination designed
primarily to secure the public interest. This
becomes three subordinate tasks: first, deciding
general rules or principles to determine pay;
second, determining how the public interest can be
served; and third, obtaining consent. The nature of
the Australian tribunals has had an enormous impact
on the way they have tackled these three questions.

The choice of wage-fixing principles is
influenced by the tribunals' long history and
judicial origins. Indeed the use of principles at
all owes much to the judicial character of the early
arbitration courts. Faced with the choice between
ad hoc and reasoned arbitration in dealing with
disputes of interests, they opted for the latter.
Using general principles to secure consistency, the
early courts established a body of published case
law that soon acquired the force of precedent.
Courts of industrial arbitration had acted much like
any other courts in establishing consistent rules to
govern their decisions.

In choosing principles the courts also betrayed
their origins. Administering 'wage justice' rather
than 'economic laws,' the tribunals leaned towards
social criteria for wage fixation. Before the First
World War a 'Basic' wage or social minimum wage was
fixed for labourers.[14] 'Margins' which fixed
the relativities for skill or other exceptional work
characteristics were settled by a mixture of
forensic investigation through work value enquiry
and fair comparison aimed at achieving comparative

wage justice. In contrast, almost no attention was paid to economic criteria for wage fixation. In these early years the economic capacity of individual employers was rarely explored since the tribunals were scarcely qualified to assess such matters. To this day, company profitability is rarely admitted as a criterion in wage fixation.

Economic considerations cannot, of course, be excluded for long when fixing pay. In Australia, tribunals began to confront these problems in the 1920s and 1930s. When they did so, they chose to examine not the economic viability of individual employers, but rather the 'capacity to pay' of the economy as a whole.[15] Once economic arguments were accepted as admissible, arbitration tribunals also had the difficult task of reconciling social and economic criteria for wage fixation. Not until 1961 did they find a solution to this problem in the 'prices and productivity' formula. By increasing wages to compensate for increases in consumer prices, the old social criterion of real wage maintenance was retained. In a growing economy, sharing productivity gains was a way of adjusting pay to take account of economic capacity. However, from the late 1960s until 1975 these principles fell into disuse as autonomous collective bargaining undermined their full application. Then in 1975 they were resuscitated in the wage indexation system.

The gradual evolution of these principles over three quarters of a century has caused them to become embedded in deep-rooted social expectations, which Isaac has termed the three conventional norms of the Australian labour market.[16] These norms are that wages should be adjusted to preserve workers' living standards, to allow them to share in growing national wealth, and to compensate particular groups for changes in work value. They coincide with the wage-fixing principles used in long-run equity-based incomes policies since 1975.

There remain two problems with them, however. First, social and economic principles for general wage fixation can still prove hard to reconcile when the economy as a whole is in recession or when particular sectors of it are doing badly. Second, principles for relative wage fixation tend to be inconsistent. In particular the stabilising principle of comparative wage justice clashes with the work value principle used to vary wage differentials. There is no principled solution to these conflicts. They reflect basic social antagonisms about income distribution. In the face of these conflicts wage-fixing principles are a fragile instrument.

Because of this the Commission has become less inclined to dictate wage-fixing principles. It now declares that it has no vested interest in any particular set of rules and seeks instead to negotiate agreement upon them.[17] National wage-fixing enquiries are increasingly a forum for bargaining and securing consent, and any presumption of a durable juristic approach to pay has given way to a sequence of temporary negotiated settlements. Underlying such bargaining is an industrial relations test. Wages principles must sustain industrial peace and will be abandoned if they fail to do so.

The second task of an incomes policy administration is to secure the public interest. Since this term defies definition,[18] the important problem is not what it means but who decides it. In Australia this question is hard to answer since responsibility for the public interest is split between the federal government and the tribunals. This divided authority is revealed in the Commonwealth Conciliation and Arbitration Act, 1904-1983 (CCAA), which provides two broad means for the public interest to be invoked. The first is by government intervention. The Minister for Industrial Relations may, for example, make submissions in national wage cases, intervene in other hearings and request a review of other tribunal decisions.[19] The second means is for the Commission on its own initiative to determine the public interest which it is required to take into account, for example, in hearings of national economic importance by paying special attention to the effects of its decisions on the level of unemployment and on inflation.[20]

Underpinning this divided authority is the judicial independence of the Commission, one of the few judicial traits which it has succeeded in formally retaining. Members of the Commission have tenure of office until the age of 65 and freedom from political direction.[21] Of course, the Commission may be dissolved by repeal of its legislation, have its statutory duties amended, or even have additional members selected for it by the government; but extreme political interference has proven electorally unpopular,[22] while light meddling is usually ineffective. History suggests that governments are best advised to persuade the

Commission rather than to interfere with it.

How does such persuasion work? Since the Commission accepts the government's right to determine economic policy, it is receptive to government economic submissions. Since 1975, national wage case decisions have rarely ignored government's suggestions as to what direction wages policy should take. Equally rarely, however, has the Commission fully implemented the government's recommendations.[23]

That the Commission and the government do not always agree may not be a bad thing for an incomes policy. It gives the Commission an aura of political neutrality which enhances its credibility with employers and unions. It also enables the Commission to shield an incomes policy from the more unrealistic or opportunistic political nostrums that emanate from politicians who do not understand industrial relations or who are more concerned with winning electoral popularity.

However, judicial independence is a twin-edged sword for incomes policy administration. As a doctrine it applies to individual tribunal members just as much as the tribunal collectively. Since incomes policy rules are not legally binding upon individual commissioners they may independently decide cases according to equity, good conscience and the substantial merits of the case.[24] Of course, appeal proceedings may allow aberrant decisions to be overturned.[25] There remains, however, a problem of ensuring consistent tribunal application of incomes policy rules. This is a less serious problem within tribunals than it is between them. The state tribunals are not obliged to follow the lead of federal tribunals; although a number of state tribunals are required to take account of national wage case decisions[26] they can still exercise their independence in ways that undermine incomes policy rules. When wage indexation broke down in 1981, for example, at least one state tribunal contributed to its demise by operating different rules to fix wage relativities.[27]

Judicial independence, then, can mean not only that governments and tribunals have different notions of the public interest, but that the tribunals cannot agree upon or apply a consistent definition themselves. The record of the past ten years suggests that such conflicts are uncommon, but when disagreements occur it is a good sign that the incomes policy is expected to achieve too wide an array of objectives and is being placed under excessive strain.

The third task is to gain consent for an incomes policy. In the first half of this century securing consent was not a great problem for the tribunals. The weakness of small unions and small employers and their dependence upon the state meant that they could rarely challenge the arbitration system. Also the courts could depend upon normal community support for the law supplemented by coercive power.[28] Like other courts, the arbitration tribunals could punish recalcitrant unions and employers by imposing orders and fines.

Since the Second World War this judicial approach has become unworkable. The independent strength of unions and employers has grown, while the tribunals' standing has fallen largely because of eccentric wage decisions.[29] In 1956 the old Arbitration Court was split, following a constitutional challenge to its power to impose penalties. The new arbitral body - the Commission - proved to be less authoritarian than its predecessor. Finally in 1969, penal sanctions against unions were dropped, after unions demonstrated that the courts had no power to collect fines.

Now, the tribunals can only operate an incomes policy by winning the support of all sides in industry. Three factors are important in this process: the tribunal's own procedures and personnel; links with unions and employer federations; and the wider political support of the federal government.

Tribunal procedures have clearly changed since the Second World War, placing more emphasis on conciliation and less upon formal arbitration. The conciliation procedures in the Act were strengthened in 1972 and 1973 to encourage this trend. The personnel of the Commission had changed too. Since 1947, the tribunal has grown in size more often through the appointment of persons with experience of industry rather than legal qualifications. Such appointments are intended to be consistent with a less legalistic and more conciliatory approach to industrial disputes. In 1972, a panel system was introduced to allow commissioners to specialise in particular industries where they could build up a stock of informal goodwill. The net effect of these changes has been to preserve a role for the Commission in an environment in which it could no longer impose its decisions.[30]

Support for an incomes policy can be harnessed directly by the Commission building close ties with the ACTU and CAI. These bodies share the Commis-

89

sion's interest in preserving a centralised system of wage fixation even though they differ over the form it should take. If they accept responsibility for incomes policy rules the problem of consent is transformed into a political problem within the ranks of these federations. Doubts are often raised about the capacity of either side to control its members. However, responsibility for incomes policy may go deeper than just the leadership of these bodies. The Commission has recently referred to the notion of 'collective responsibility' - an idea that articulates a widespread if not universal ideology founded in a collectivist labour movement operating in a highly regulated economy.[31] This ideology spreads well outside the top leadership of industrial relations professionals and finds expression in political policies which support centralised labour market regulation allied to state, social and economic protectionism. The idea of collective responsibility is now deeply engrained in Australia, and enables both the ACTU and CAI to enlist support for an incomes policy from many of their affiliates.

Third, governments must play a strong role in winning consent with an incomes policy. Surprisingly, despite traditional heavy involvement in both economic and social welfare, governments stood aloof from incomes policy until the mid-1970s, leaving the Commission to depend upon its own powers of persuasion. Such a policy may have recognised the formal independence of the tribunals; it became untenable, however, after the collapse of the Commission's prestige in the period from 1965 to 1974. In the early 1970s wage determination and industrial relations became problem areas. Consequently, the government found intervention unavoidable.

Incomes policies since then have depended heavily upon the bargaining power of the government. For example, the government can trade concessions in such areas as taxation, price surveillance, government spending, the general level of economic activity, manpower policy, health and education to extract compliance with an incomes policy. Wage indexation in 1975 was constructed on such a foundation. The Accord too is a deal covering a wide range of policy areas besides incomes. One result of this 'social contract bargaining' is that incomes policies have become less concerned with award wages than with the 'social wage' - a term that highlights the net effect of government charges and subsidies upon real disposable incomes.[32]

The paradox of Australian incomes policies is that they are negotiated devices clothed in the formal institutional trappings of compulsory arbitration. But behind the actual forms of adversarial proceedings before independent tribunals lies the political reality that governments, tribunals, unions and employers must all agree if an incomes policy is to work for long. A major source of strength for Australian incomes policies has been the Commission's experience with wage-fixing principles, its independence, and its skill and acceptability in oiling negotiations.

WAGE INDEXATION, 1975-1981

Wage indexation was introduced as a corrective to the inflationary collective bargaining system that had grown up in the 1960s and early 1970s. The preceding system was usually described as a three-tier system since it allowed wage adjustment at three different levels - the nation, industry and workplace.[33] These three tiers were poorly co-ordinated with each other. As a result, it was possible that their cumulative effect could be highly inflationary.

In 1973-4, Australia's inflation rate increased alarmingly. This was connected with the oil price shock, escalating world commodity prices and expanding government expenditure. However, it was also a consequence of an overheated labour market in which the institutional forces governing pay were incapable of instilling restraint.[34] Table 2 shows movements in key economic measures including productivity, earnings, prices, unemployment and industrial disputes. From this it is clear that in 1973-4 real wages surged ahead of productivity movements, creating what was termed 'real wage overhang', a phenomenon that allegedly encouraged capital labour substitution with damaging consequences for Australia's unemployment level for the rest of the decade.[35] At the same time, disordered wage fixation was connected with a large increase in industrial disputes in the years 1969-74. This was another reason for taking a critical look at the three-tier system and finding, if possible, an alternative.

A Labour government had won the federal elections in December of 1972. Initially it was committed to extending collective bargaining in place

Australia: New Wine Into Old Bottles

Table 2 - Production, Earnings, Prices, Unemployment
& Industrial Disputes
1967-1976 (1967 = 100)

	G.D.P. at Constant Prices per person employed	Average Male Weekly Earnings (Adult Males)	Consumer Prices	Unemployment %	Number of Industrial Disputes
1967	100	100	100	1.4	1,340
1968	101.0	106.8	103.3	1.3	1,713
1969	107.9	114.6	106.0	1.0	2,014
1970	109.3	123.8	109.4	0.9	2,738
1971	110.5	138.7	114.6	1.2	2,404
1972	112.7	148.8	122.4	1.7	2,298
1973	114.3	175.1	129.8	1.4	1,538
1974	118.7	225.2	146.6	1.3	2,809
1975	120.9	250.2	171.1	4.0	2,432
1976	123.2	283.7	193.3	4.3	2,055

of compulsory arbitration, an approach inconsistent with incomes policy. However, in 1973, alarmed by rising prices, the government unsuccessfully sought, by referendum, to acquire constitutional power to control wages and prices directly. Having failed to secure the legal basis for direct incomes control, the government turned to other measures.

In July, 1974, Clyde Cameron, the Minister for Labour, proposed that the Commission should link wages to increases in consumer prices. His policy was weakened when he insisted, in the interests of both equality and inflation control, that full indexation should only be given to the lower paid. The idea could not win trade union support. Exploratory conferences chaired by the President of the Arbitration Commission failed to get any agreement on such a system.

However, in November, 1974, the Commission opened an inquiry into a claim by the ACTU for full wage indexation. The ACTU asked initially that full indexation should supplement collective bargaining, not supplant it. The Commission was unwilling to apply such a system. Only after the ACTU conceded that wage increases be confined to indexation rises, except in rare and isolated cases, did the Commission agree to experiment with a centralised incomes policy.[37]

Wage indexation consisted of a set of rules to control wage determination. These rules fell into three types: rules governing the general level of pay; rules governing wage relativities; and rules to enforce the incomes policy. Of the first type, Principle 1 of the wage-fixing guidelines was the most important. It stated that:

> The Commission will adjust its award wages and salaries each quarter in relation to the most recent movement of the six-capitals CPI unless it is persuaded to the contrary by those seeking to oppose the judgement.

This principle set the pattern for the next six years. It did two things; it created an expectation that the value of real wages would be preserved, and it provided an opportunity for debate upon whether or not full indexation would be granted. Between 1975 and 1981, the choice between full and partial wage indexation was the most important point of discussion in wage determination.

Table 3 shows the indexation decisions made in national wage cases between 1975 and 1981. It is apparent that 'full indexation' was the exception and not the rule.

Table 3 – Wage Indexation Decisions, 1975–1981

Date		CPI Variation (%)	Wage Variation
1975	March	3.6	3.6%
	June	3.5	3.5%
	September	0.8	NIL
	December	5.6	(5.6% + 0.8%) = 6.4%
1976	March	3.0	3.0% to $125 per week, $3.80 thereafter.
	June	2.5	2.5% to $98 per week, then $2.50 to $98–$166 per week, 1.5% thereafter.
	September	2.2	2.2%
	December	6.0	$5.70
1977	March	2.3	1.9% to $2.00 per week, $3.80 thereafter.

Table 3 (cont'd)

Date		CPI Variation (%)	Wage Variation
	June	2.4	2.0%
	September	2.0	1.5%
	December	2.3	1.5% to $170 per week, $2.60 thereafter.
1978	March	1.3	1.3%
	June/September	4.0	4.0%
1979	December (78)/March	4.0	3.2%
	June/September	5.0	4.5%
1980	December (79)/March	5.3	4.2%
	June/September	4.7	3.7%
1981	December (80)/March	4.5	3.6%

Source: National Case decisions. From June/September, 1978 the frequency of hearings was changed from four a year to two a year.

Unions accepted the system in 1975, expecting to be granted full indexation. In fact, this occurred in only six of the nineteen cases over the six year period. Partial indexation, more than anything else, caused unions to seek supplementary wage increases outside the indexation guidelines, particularly once the economy had begun to recover in 1978-9.

The action of the Commission in awarding partial indexation was largely a response to Government submissions, although, as Table 4 shows, the Liberal/National party government that came to office in November, 1975, would have preferred a far more drastic cut in real wages.

Table 4 - Commonwealth Wage Submissions
June Quarter, 1975 - June September Quarters, 1980

Quarter		CPI Movement (%)	Proposed Wage Increase (%)
1975	June	3.5	3.5
	September	0.8	Nil or 0.8
	December	6.4	3.2
1976	March	3.0	Flat $2.80
	June	2.5	Nil or 0.75
	September	2.2	About 0.6
	December	6.0 Health 3.2	Flat $2.90
		Other 2.8	Nil
1977	March	2.3	Nil
	June	2.4	Nil
	September	2.0	Nil
	December	2.3	Nil
1978	March	1.3	Nil
	June/September	4.0	Nil or small percentage
	December/March	4.0	Nil
1979	June/September	5.0	3.0
	December/March	5.3	Nil
1980	June/September	4.7	Nil

Instead, the Commission steered a middle road between union demands for full indexation and government demands for nil indexation. Although aware that union support for the system would eventually be eroded by partial indexation, the Commission felt it had no alternative, given that Section 39(2) of the Commonwealth Conciliation and Arbitration Act required it to consider the effects of its decisions upon inflation and unemployment. The existence of tight monetary policies for much of the late 1970s meant, in the Commission's view, that full indexation could exacerbate unemployment. On this reasoning, partial indexation was unavoidable. After 1978, partial indexation was based mainly on government claims that CPI increases be discounted for the effects of increases in indirect taxes. Again, the Commission felt it had no alternative but to discount CPI movements since to do otherwise would be to work contrary to government economic policy.

The second principle for varying the general level of wages was Principle 6 which allowed increases on account of national productivity. This proved, in comparison with Principle 1, to be of no value. No productivity cases were held throughout the life of wage indexation.

Wage relativities could be changed in two main ways. Under Principle 4, national wage case decisions could be framed in such a way as to compress vertical differentials across the entire work force. The Commission had a choice between awarding tapered indexation decisions, which had this effect, or uniform percentage CPI adjustments, which maintained wage differentials as they were. This principle was employed extensively in 1976 and 1977 when four out of seven CPI adjustments were tapered, effectively compressing wage differentials. This caused some discontent among white collar unions. Following an inquiry into wage-fixing principles in 1978, the Commission placated these unions by deciding that discounting would in future only be done by giving uniform percentage wage increases of less the full CPI movement.

The second way to vary relativities was to single out particular groups as exceptional cases meriting a pay increase. Initially, Principle 7 provided two variations of this method. First, Principle 7(a) allowed for 'work value' cases to be mounted where the skill or responsibility needed for a particular task had changed. Second, Principle 7(b) allowed for those who had been held back in the 1974 wage round to catch up on the community movement. Additional grounds for exceptional treatment were added as the indexation package grew older.

In May, 1976, Principle 7(c) was included to deal with 'anomalies.' Under this principle, arguments about 'anomalies' (which remained undefined) could be heard privately (to discourage comparability claims), after the central union and employer federations had agreed that an anomaly existed. These hearings were termed 'Anomalies Conferences.' Where the two sides disagreed, a Full Bench of the Commission had to hear the claim to ensure that it was legitimate. Comparative wage justice arguments could not be used to demonstrate an anomaly and if any risk of a 'flow-on' to others was detected the tribunals were reluctant to grant a wage increase. Finally, in 1978, Principle 7(d) was added to deal with 'inequities' where workers doing similar work received dissimilar rates of pay. The procedure for rectifying an 'inequity' was the same as that for an 'anomaly.'

These principles worked as a pressure release valve, allowing claims for exceptional treatment. Of the four principles, 7(a) was the weakest and became the most abused. A work value wage round took place between 1977 and 1980, giving a wage increase to everyone, rather than just those whose work value could be shown to have changed. In 1977, an aircraft industry work value case was held arising largely out of new work routines that followed the introduction of wide-bodied aircraft. In accordance with Principle 7(a), only some classifications in the award could be given the wage increase, not all. The decision to do this created discontent amongst those workers who received no pay increase. As a result, the following March, they were levelled up to their more fortunate colleagues by a process called 'averaging.' Subsequently, comparability claims spread the work value wage round across the entire workforce. In 1979, the Metal Industry Award, Australia's largest award, was increased by $7.30 for non-tradesmen and $13.30 for tradesmen. Salaried workers generally received about a 4% wage increase. In 1980 the stable door was closed after the horse had bolted. Principle 7(a) was amended to prevent 'averaging.' This would prevent future work value wage increases sparking a general round.

The other criteria for exceptional treatment were not eroded by comparative wage justice claims. Principle 7(b) on community catch-up expired in 1976 and was finally buried in 1978. The 'anomalies' and 'inequities' principles, by their very design, could not be converted into an excuse for a general wage movement.

Finally, the wage indexation principles contained enforcement rules. The Commission adopted indexation in 1975 on the clear condition that it could be abandoned if significant additional wage movements occurred. From this evolved the practice in each national wage case of testing for 'substantial compliance.' To do this, the Commission looked at evidence of earnings movements and industrial disputes. The first would indicate whether wage drift had occurred. The second would indicate whether pressure was being placed on employers to break the guidelines.

The employers generally argued that lack of compliance should be punished by either deferring a hearing, or granting only partial indexation. However, the Commission rarely took a punitive course of action in national wage cases. In two

instances the Commission claimed that discounting
occurred partly because of the effects of industrial
disputes. For example, in November, 1977, a 2.0%
price increase was discounted by 0.5% on account of
'the state of the economy, the economic effects of
recent strikes and stoppages, and for price increases attributable to devaluation.'   In July,
1980, the 4.7% CPI increase was discounted to a 3.7%
wage increase, in part because of industrial disputes.

If 'across the board' discounting was too crude
a sanction, the Commission could instead withhold
national wage case increases from particular male-
factors.   In the 1978 review of wage-fixing principles, the Commission argued:

> It would be reluctant to withhold an increase
> from the working community generally if an
> identifiable section was creating problems.
> However, we see no reason why individual
> members of the Commission, given appropriate
> circumstances, should not withhold increases in
> particular industries or establishments.[38]

This sanction too was used sparingly, being
confined to a small number of instances, in the
building industry for example, in 1976 and 1977.
Indeed, the whole idea that sanctions might enforce
compliance with the principles never appears to have
been very important in practice.   The Commission
insisted instead that the survival of wage indexation rested upon voluntary support, a notion quite
at variance with the idea of compulsion.

Such voluntary support appears to have been
forthcoming.   Unions generally were content to
accept the wage indexation system, making most of
its benefits and observing its rules.   Indicative of
this acceptance was the very high proportion of wage
increases that came from national wage case decisions.   Table 5 shows how, from 1975 to 1980, wage
indexation accounted for more than 85% of the
increases in male wages, and more than 95% of female
wage increases.   This was telling evidence for compliance.   Equally, the declining ratio of wage
indexation increases to total wage increases in
1980-1, testified to the growing ineffectiveness of
the policy.   The Commission's response to this was
to threaten to terminate the wage indexation
system.

Australia: New Wine Into Old Bottles

Table 5 - Wage Indexation Increases as a Percentage
of Change in Total Wage, Australia, 1975 to 1981

Year End	Male (%)	Female (%)
August, 1976	92	94
August, 1977	94	96
June, 1978	98	99
December, 1978	89	97
June, 1979	86	95
January, 1980	86	96
July, 1980	81	86
January, 1981	83	70
May, 1981	91	79

Source: Australian Bureau of Statistics
Wage Rate Index (Preliminary)
Cat. No. 6311.0

Wage indexation hovered upon the brink of
extinction upon a number of separate occasions. In
June, 1979, the Commission threatened to end the
system, claiming of the unions and employers, that
'one wants indexation without restraints and the
other wants restraints without indexation.'[39]
On this occasion the threat was withdrawn. Eighteen
months later, the Commission had clearly tired of
the task of policing an incomes policy that seemed
unwelcome to unions and employers. In January,
1981, the Commission came back to the brink,
announcing that no more wage hearings would be heard
under the old principles, and that a review would
take place. The Commission argued:

> In addition to our concern about the level of
> industrial disputes, we are firmly of the view
> that underlying the persistent difficulties in
> operating the principles are strongly
> conflicting and irreconcilable expectations
> among the major participants before us about
> the objectives of the system.[40]

The review that took place in March failed to
produce agreement upon a new centralised system, and

the Commission was unable to elicit suggestions for
an orderly decentralised system. The following
month, the last national wage case hearing occurred
under the indexation rules, awarding 80% of the CPI
increase to the unions, with the promise that the
remaining 20% could be 'topped up' at the next
hearing at the end of the year. There was no
subsequent hearing. Several wage disputes erupted
in July. Unable to resolve them within the guidelines, or prevent the employers and unions negotiating, the Commission terminated wage indexation.
On July 31, 1981, the President of the Commission,
Sir John Moore, noted:

> The events since April have shown quite clearly
> that the commitment of the participants to the
> system is not strong enough to sustain the
> requirements for its continued operation.

What brought wage indexation to an end? Formally, the reason given was the failure of unions
and employers to support the system. This begs the
question of why such support evaporated when it did.
Two competing explanations gained widespread support.

First, the unions argued that they were tired
of partial indexation which had eroded real wages.
Between 1975 and 1981, wage indexation had been the
main source of wage increases for most workers. The
'work value' round of 1977-1980 had been the only
major addition to this. No productivity case had
taken place. Resentment against partial indexation
finally exploded in a rash of claims. In 1980-1
unions in the metal trades campaigned effectively
for working hours to be reduced from 40 to 35 per
week. In early 1981, a rash of wage claims in
railways, telecommunications, road transport and
other industries, were conducted outside the guidelines. Much of this activity was justified as
compensation for the wage restraint imposed by the
Commission since 1976.

The second explanation turned upon the effects
of the economic recovery associated with the
'Resources Boom' anounced by the Prime Minister in
the 1980 federal election. The boom was only felt
in some regions, such as the Hunter Valley, where
coal, metal mining and mining-support industries
were important. However, the upward pressure on
wages created by strong labour demand and union
bargaining power could not be isolated to these
regions.

It is probable that both explanations were partially valid. However, they differed in their policy implications, the first suggesting that a 'fair' indexation system would have survived any economic upturn, and the second hinting at the intrinsic vulnerability of any incomes policy to a decline in the market discipline of unemployment.

A third explanation was put forward by Mr. R.J. Hawke, who in 1981 had freshly retired as president of the ACTU to take up a political career. He explained the breakdown of wage indexation as a consequence of the closure of the Prices Justification Tribunal (PJT) in early 1981. Wage restraint without price restraint, it was argued, was unacceptable to trade unions. Since the wage fixation system provided retroactive price compensation to incomes, his argument appeared spurious. However, it did loosely suggest an important reason why unions lost faith in indexation. This was the abandonment of the supporting mechanisms which made the system acceptable. When the ACTU accepted indexation in 1975, it did so with the proviso that tax scales be indexed, price surveillance operated, and that equitable economic and social policies be applied. Wage indexation was, in short, part of a general package of social and economic measures negotiated between unions and the government. The deal expired when the Australian Labour party government lost office in November, 1975. The Fraser government that came into power gradually cut away all these supporting mechanisms, the last one being price justification. Although the PJT had become moribund some years before, its closure signified how government policy had drifted away from the compact made in 1975.

It is usual now to blame the Liberal/National party federal government for the breakdown of wage indexation. By persistently demanding partial indexation, and removing supporting economic and social policies, the government placed wage indexation under impossible strain. Indeed, the achievement of the Commission was to keep indexation in place for so long when the political and economic climate was so adverse.

There is some evidence that indexation in some degree succeeded in improving the trade-off between inflation and unemployment. Table 6 shows that movements in earnings, wage rates and prices in 1975-80 were much lower than movements in the periods 1973-75 and 1980-82, when decentralised wage-fixing systems were in operation.

Table 6 - Prices & Wages, 1960-1984

	Average Earnings	Minimum Wage Rates	Consumer Prices
1960-1970	5.7	4.1	2.5
1970-1973	10.7	11.3	6.7
1973-1975	20.5	24.0	15.1
1975-1980	10.9	10.2	10.7
1980-1982	13.8	12.0	10.5
1982-1984	8.5	6.0	6.3

Source: Hancock Committee of Review, Report, Vol. II, p. 81.

The connection between indexation and lower wage and price movements in 1975-80 may of course be coincidental, not causal. Disentangling the impact of incomes policy from other independent variables remains an elusive task. The Hancock Committee summed up the problem as arising from:

> The inherent difficulty of demonstrating any proposition as to what the state of things would have been if some alternative path had been trodden.[41]

Despite this, some work had been done to separate the economic results of incomes policy. Phipps' monetarist model estimated what wage movements would have been in the absence of an incomes policy, if they had have been based on expectations sourced in actual wage behaviour in preceding periods. He found that wage indexation slowed down wage-price movements until the second quarter of 1977.[42] He argued, however, that after mid-1977 indexation isolated real wages from the effects of excess supply in the labour market, preventing wage inflation falling as fast as it might have done.

Such findings coincide with casual empiricism. The educated guess of a number of economists has been that money wages (or money wages deflated by the CPI) would have increased more rapidly over 1975-1979 if the pre-1975 wage system had continued and indexation had not been introduced.[43] On the other hand, the Federal Treasury persisted in arguing that indexation propped up money wages, whose rate of increase would have fallen more rapidly in the depressed labour market of the late 1970s.[44]

THE CASE-BY-CASE SYSTEM, AUGUST, 1981-DECEMBER, 1982

When the Commission terminated wage indexation, the wage-fixing principles were only partly revoked. Although there were to be no more national wage cases to consider price and productivity increases, the supporting principles prohibiting comparative wage justice claims remained in force. This meant that the Commission, if forced to arbitrate or ratify agreements, would not transmit comparability pressures, but would consider each claim, case by case, upon its individual merits.

Since the Commission had given up restricting pay increases, restraint, so the government and Treasury claimed, would be sustained by employers whose resistance would be stiffened by a tight monetary policy in the private sector and strict budgetary controls in the public sector. While there were no targets or guidelines for the outcome of negotiations, the general economic climate was intended to restrict decentralised bargaining.

In general, the tribunals were now freed of the task of administering an incomes policy, and could perform their usual functions of resolving disputes by conciliation and arbitration. They continued, however, to police agreements in certain areas. Of these, the most important was standard hours. The 35-hour-week campaign that had sprung up in 1979-80 had yielded several successes. The Commission, before it would vary awards to less than forty hours a week, was required to form a Full Bench to hear such claims, and adopted the practice of requiring cost offsets to justify the reduction.

The intention of the system was to allow employers and unions to negotiate diverse settlements depending upon the economic capacity of different sections of industry. Several things went wrong with this approach. For one thing, the state tribunals continued to award across the board pay increases. The New South Wales Industrial Commission awarded a CPI increase of 4.3% in January, 1982 to awards that had not been adjusted in a significant manner since the end of indexation. Queensland and Western Australia lifted their state minimum wages by a flat $6.30 in late 1981. In early 1982, Victoria and Tasmania levelled all state awards up to the metal trades standard. The case-by-case approach only applied to that 35% of the workforce under federal awards.

Second, the ACTU campaigned to obtain the metal trades standard in all federal awards, orchestrating a sequence of co-ordinated negotiations in all the major industries. The metal trades standard was the result of an agreement reached in the metal trades in December, 1981, which set out several major conditions. There was an immediate wage increase of $25.00 for the metal tradesman, along with $9.30 increase in allowances and a 'mid-term adjustment' of $14.00 for the tradesman, to be paid in June, 1982 to cover anticipated increases in the CPI. Standard hours would be reduced from 40 to 38 as well. Meanwhile, the unions undertook to make no further claims for the duration of the agreement. A virtually identical agreement was settled in the building industy the same month.

Since the two awards were the largest in terms of employee coverage, they set a pattern for future negotiations. Labour cost increases were substantial. For example, the hourly rate of the building trades craftsmen rose by 26.1% under the terms of the agreement. Alarming though the size of these increases was, the government did not oppose them in the public interest and the Commission duly endorsed them.

The ACTU pressed its claim to standardise federal award movements in a national wage case that was completed in May, 1982. The ACTU asked for centralised wage determination to be resumed, and for all employees to be levelled up to the metal trades standard. The government and the CAI opposed both applications successfully. The evidence submitted to the hearing made it clear that the case-by-case system was only a partial success. For example, in a survey of 127 federal and state awards, 'fair comparability' had been the only ground for an increase in 22% of cases, while it had been a partial justification in 72% of cases. Moreover, a substantial minority had kept pace with the metal trades award. More than 20% of the sample had negotiated both a wage increase of more than $20.00 and a mid-term adjustment. These awards covered just a third of employees in the sample. On the other hand, 33% of awards covering 8.7% of the sampled employees had risen by less than $20.00 and had no mid-term adjustment. Moreover, about 20% of employees covered by federal and state awards had received no wage increase of any kind since the end of indexation. The case-by-case system had neither suppressed comparability arguments nor stopped unions targetting wage movements upon the generous metal trades standard. All that it had done was to lag the speed of comparability adjustments.

The ACTU claim was, in effect, deferred rather than rejected. In December, 1982, the Commission agreed to resume centralised wage determination and allowed claims for unions to catch up to the metal trades standard. Ironically, this decision accompanied the imposition of a wage freeze, to be applied to all new claims including the fresh round of wage negotiations that were being conducted in the metal, building, transport and storage industries.

Alarmed by rapidly rising unemployment, the federal government called a conference of state premiers in early December to discuss a wage freeze. The agreement was gained from all states, the freeze was imposed, curtailing the round of wage bargains. At one stroke, those at the front of the wages race were called to a halt, while those in the rear could, with difficulty, catch up. Belated claims for the metal trades standard faced several difficulties, however. Most important was the reluctance of the Commission to place a percentage figure on that standard. Instead, the Commission tended to interpret it as comprising an initial pay increase and a mid-term adjustment. Clearly this left scope for wide inter-award variance. To a degree this practice betrayed the principle that award movements in 1981-2 should be retrospectively standardised.

The outcome of all this was that the case-by-case system produced much less flexibility than was intended. Worse, the cost shock of the metal trades standard - up to 30% increase in labour costs - had contributed to a dramatic upturn in inflation in 1982, and an increase in unemployment from 5.8% in 1981 to 7.2 % in 1982 and 10.0% in 1983. A further drawback was that several groups who had not caught up on the full value of the metal trades standard were resentful, and their claims were to bring future industrial trouble. Among this group were transport workers, who had not gained the 38-hour week, and federal public servants, whose pay had fallen behind both state public servants and most manual workers.

If one seeks indications of how much flexibility was achieved in this period, perhaps most important were the lags in wage adjustment. Some groups - notably federal public servants - were not to catch up on the 1981-2 wage round until the middle of 1985. There was also considerable diversity in the size of wage increases. Finally, the tribunals succeeded in preventing a general community movement to reduce standard hours.

If the objective of the ACTU had been to obtain a rough-and-ready approximation to the gains that indexation would have achieved in 1981-2, the case-by-case system probably yielded far more varied results than they would have liked. Equally, the wage explosion at the end of 1981 meant that the system was far from satisfactory to the government and employers, and retrospective standardisation whittled away that flexibility sought by the policy.

THE WAGE FREEZE, DECEMBER, 1982-JUNE, 1983

Centralised wage determinaton was resumed with the imposition of a wage freeze in December, 1982. The rationale for the freeze, in the judgement delivered by the Commission on 23 December, was the need to restrain wages so as to offset the rising unemployment attributable to severe world recession, a prolonged local drought affecting primary industries, and the wages explosion.

Although the federal and state governments agreed upon the need for a wage freeze, its duration was more controversial. Three states - New South Wales, South Australia and Victoria - sought a six-month pause. The federal government and the other three states wanted a twelve-month freeze.

To the extent that this question lay in the hands of the various governments, they could, and did, pursue different courses. The West Australian Salaries and Wage Freeze Act, for example, froze public service pay in that state for a year. In contrast, the Commonwealth Salaries and Wage Pause Act (1982), and the Tasmanian Employment (Stabilisation of Remuneration) Act, 1982, only applied for six months.

In the private sector, however, the federal and state governments had to persuade their industrial tribunals both that a freeze was needed, and that it should last for a particular period. The Commonwealth Commission set the lead by taking a 'wait-and-see' approach, reviewing the wage freeze after six months. The other state tribunals took the same approach, although the Victorian Industrial Relations Commission did not announce its decision until the middle of February, by which time a third of the freeze period had expired.

Such delays were of little significance. There was almost no independent bargaining pressure to increase pay. The major concern of most unions was to keep check upon an avalanche of redundancies. To this end, the New South Wales government passed the Employment Protection Act in December, 1982, requiring employers to notify both unions and the Industrial Commission of substantial redundancies. Perhaps more important, several tribunals established scales of redundancy payment in a sequence of decisions beginning in early 1983.

How did the freeze work? In the March quarter of 1982, male earnings rose by only 1.0%. In the June quarter, the increase was 0.7%. Female earnings rose even more sluggishly. That there was any rise at all was largely attributed to changes in the composition of the survey sample brought about by the higher rate of retrenchment amongst the lower-paid unskilled workers. In short, the freeze was closely adhered to. Nor was there a subsequent wage explosion to compensate. In effect, the metal trades standard had been spread over an additional six month period. This amounted to a clawback of real labour costs, although the 29.8% hourly increase for the metal tradesmen in December, 1981, still represented a substantial gain against the 19.0% increase in consumer prices over the period between the two indexation systems. Briefly, real wages fell back, as consumer prices rose by 4.3% in the first two quarters of 1983, providing some respite for employers.

One difficulty with the wage freeze was finding a workable wage-fixing system to take its place. The Fraser government had turned its back upon wage indexation, but equally had repudiated the case-by-case approach. It did not appear capable of leading negotiations to find a new wage-fixing system. In March, 1983, this problem was solved when the government was defeated by the Australian Labour party led by Mr. Bob Hawke. Part of the new government's mandate was to establish another incomes policy.

PHASE IV: THE PRICES AND INCOMES ACCORD SINCE 1983

The 'Accord' contained three important elements. First, government economic policy was to be based upon an incomes policy in which centralised wage fixation linked pay to prices and productivity. Second, the quid pro quo for union wage restraint was a network of supporting social and economic policies covering industrial relations, industry development, migration, social security, occupational health and safety, education, health, and government employment. Third, the government was to employ a style of 'open government' involving unions, employers, and other interst groups in consultation and decision making, and giving them free access to government information for this purpose. Government was to be by 'consensus.'

The policy was first settled between the Australian Labour party and the ACTU in February, 1983, following several years of sluggish negotiation. The following month it became government policy when the Labour party led by Bob Hawke won a federal election, largely on the strength of its promises about the Accord. In April, the new government convened a summit conference to draw leading employers and state governments into a pact which was still, to that time, agreed only between unions and government. The summit was a public triumph for the Government. Although nominally about general economic strategy, the key matter under discussion was wages policy. Government offered three options, constructed so that the middle ground was their own preferred option. This provided for a 3% wage rise in 1983, full wage indexation in 1984, and a productivity case in 1985. The momentum of the government carried the day, and a summit communique that endorsed its preferred option gained near-unanimous support. Two conservative state premiers - from Queensland and Tasmania - remained aloof.

The major points in the communique were as follows. Centralised determination based on prices and productivity would be resumed. Second, real wage maintenance would be deferred in 1983 because of the economic crisis, and other claims by unions would be suppressed except in special or extraordinary circumstances. The centralised system would be proposed to the Commission, which was not represented at the summit, at a special conference. Finally, union wage claims would take into account changes in the 'social wage' brought about by government expenditure.

After the wage freeze had expired at the end of June, discussions began before the Commission to establish a new incomes policy. On 23 September, these talks bore fruit when the Commission announced both a 4.3% wage increase based upon CPI movements, and the adoption of a fresh set of centralised wage-fixing principles.

The new wage-fixing principles were very much like the wage indexation guidelines. There were, however, three small areas of novelty. First, the criteria for exceptional cases had been extended, not to give more flexibility, but to control areas that the old guidelines had not dealt with explicitly. Most important here were the restrictions upon agreements to reduce standard hours of work, and rules governing supplementary payments and 'paid rates awards' (which specified a maximum as well as a minimum wage). Second, the Commission adopted a test in cases where unions were seeking improved conditions of employment requiring that such improvements cause negligible cost increases. Third, there was a new enforcement rule. Under Principle 3 of the guidelines, unions seeking to gain national wage case pay increases had to apply individually before the Commission, and guarantee that they would not pursue any extra claims except in accordance with the principles.

The new enforcement rule was a major innovation. In practice it came to mean that unions had to give evidence that either their members or their governing bodies had agreed that there be no further claims. Almost immediately, this provision was put to the test. Unions in the building industry had negotiated a wage increase of around $20.00 just before the new guidelines came into effect, but had not been able to get the award varied to incorporate the increase. Building workers had been led to expect the pay rise, but the Commission could not allow it since it failed to comply with the grounds for exception contained in the new principles. The 4.3% wage increase was deferred in that industry. Meanwhile, several building unions operated work bans to force the employers to pay both the $20.00 and the 4.3%. Finally, a settlement was reached in which the Commission disguised a pay increase as superannuation contributions. As in the late 1970s, the most turbulent unions, whose behaviour was likely to upset the system, were those in the building industry.

Others seeking exceptional treatment were white collar workers who had been left behind in the wage round of 1981-2, and whom the freeze had prevented from catching up. If they wished to obtain the metal trades standard, they had to lodge claims to establish an 'equitable base' by December, 1983. The first such claims to be settled came from university

and college lecturers, whose pay had only risen by
13% in 1981-2, well behind both inflation and the
community movement.   In April, 1984 the Academic
Salaries Tribunal - their independent arbitral body
- awarded a 5% wage increase to them.   This created
an expectation that the numerically more significant
group that was next in the queue - the lower levels
of the Federal Public Service - would get a similar
increase.   When the Commission heard their case in
early 1985, it baulked at increasing pay for so many
employees.   The claim was rejected.   Subsequently,
work bans were imposed which disrupted tax collec-
tion and other government activities.   The ACTU
pressed successfully to have the case reheard, and
wage increases of 2% to 3-1/2% were finally granted
in May, 1985.

The fear with such cases was that they would
set a precedent to which other workers would claim
entitlement.   Two factors appeared important in
resisting such flow-on pressures.   First, the
wage-fixing guidelines formally prohibited flow-on
from 'equitable base' cases.   The Commission backed
up this rule by extracting promises from the unions
that each case was unique.   Second, the ACTU was
able to police the system to exclude some bogus
claims.

Nonetheless, the problem of some wage seepage -
pay increases in addition to national wage case
increases - was more serious than at the beginning
of the wage indexation system in 1975.   At that
time, wage indexation had been imposed when a wage
explosion had freshly occurred, the economy was
going into recession, and unemployment was rising.
These factors discouraged demands for additional
wage increases.   In contrast, the Accord arrived
after a lengthy wage freeze, and when the economy
was beginning to recover.

One outlet for wage pressure were the 'anomalies conferences' where claims were lodged to
rectify anomalies and inequities, and to establish
an equitable base for indexation to apply.   Between
October, 1983 and December, 1984, 205 anomalies and
inequities claims were heard.   Of these, 29 (14%)
were rejected either by the conference or a Full
Bench of the Commission; 56 (27%) were stood over or
a final decision was not handed down; 120 (58%) were
resolved by an adjustment.   It is clear that there
was little uniformity in the treatment of anomalies,
except in cases seeking the metal trades standard.
The Commission was not reluctant to throw out
dubious claims, and moreover, most cases involved

small groups of workers. In short, this fell well short of a general wage movement.

There were fewer 'work value' claims made in the same period, but more of them were resolved in the union's favour. Of 47 claims, only 4 (8.5%) were refused directly; 3 (6.4%) were referred back to the parties for discussion; in 7 (14.9%) cases an allowance was approved, while in 6 (12.8%) cases a direct wage increase was granted. In the largest category, 27 (57.5%) cases were resolved by reclassification or regrading. Improvements in earnings resulted in 40 (85%) of the cases.[45]

Allowances were another area where the unions made substantial gains. Of 66 claims to vary site allowances in the building industry, 44 (66.6%) were approved and 22 (33.3%) were rejected. Of 115 other allowance claims, 95 (82.6%) were granted, while only 9 (7.8%) were refused. A further 11 (9.5%) were not settled.

Finally, in the same period, about 50 claims were made for reduction in standard working hours. Although the number of cases was not large, several of the awards were large ones. Reductions to 38 hours occurred in textiles, clothing, footwear, timber, the blue collar sector of public employment, hotels and railways. The agreements in these cases were closely monitored by the Commission, which required cost offsets. This led the federal government to conclude that the cost effects of reduced hours had been kept to a minimum. However, it is likely that the impact of concessions here would have been greater than that of pay increases arising from anomalies, work value and allowance claims.

The changes in earnings discussed so far occurred within the Commission's wage-fixing principles. In mid-1985, concern began to be voiced that earnings drift was occurring outside the Commission. Dawkins and Blandy argued that in the year to November of 1984 earnings increased by 2.7% more than award rates. Eliminating the effect of additional overtime, they calculated 2.0% wage drift over the period.[46] To a small degree some drift could be expected since the Commission allowed, under Principle 1(d), that over-award payments might be indexed to preserve earnings relativities. Such increases would, by definition, be recorded as wage drift, even though fully in accordance with the Commission's wage-fixing rules. It is not possible, therefore, to condemn all wage drift as non-compliance with the centralised system. More generally,

there are difficulties in measuring earnings drift
in Australia which pose difficulties for policy
prescriptions based upon often slight movements in
the measured earnings-wage gap.

Notwithstanding all these signs of additional
pay or labour cost movements, it appears possible to
conclude that the Accord is holding up as an incomes
policy. This has happened despite the strong
economic recovery since 1983. One reason why unions
have been generally content to restrict their claims
to national wage case increases, has been the record
of full indexation delivered since September, 1983.
Table 7 shows CPI movements and national case
decisions since 1983.

Table 7 - National Wage Case Decisions

1983 - 1985

		CPI%	NWC%
March/June quarters	1983	4.3	4.3
September/December quarters	1983	4.1	4.1
March/June quarters	1984	-0.2	deferred
September/December quarters	1984	2.7	2.7
March/June quarters	1985	3.8	3.8

In economic terms, the performance of the
Accord has been considered impressive. It enabled
price movements and wage movements to be pulled down
to a very low level in 1984 - a year in which GDP
grew by 6.0% while employment expanded by 3.0%.
While much of this growth can be attributed to
recovery from a very low trough in 1982-3, the
Accord succeeded in holding back wage pressures.

A particular piece of sleight-of-hand played a
large part in the low wage and price movements of
that year. A shift in medical insurance from private expenditure to direct taxation produced a
negative CPI movement at the beginning of the year.
To compensate for the Medicare levy which taxpayers
had to meet, the Government gave most wage earners a
cut in income tax of the order of $7.60 a week.
Thus wage restraint was cemented by the adroit use
of fiscal policy.

In August, 1985, the government looked again at
ways of holding back national wage case increases.
The reason for this was a serious run on the

Australian dollar facilitated by a decision to float the exchange rate, and prompted by a serious and prolonged balance of payments deficit in 1984-5. The decline of the dollar against not only the American dollar, but also the yen and sterling, created a demand in financial circles that wage discounting was needed to hold back Australian labour costs so that exporters could capitalise on their competitive advantage. This would be seen as a step to resolve the balance of payments problem. Failure to take such action would, the government feared, cause a speculative run on the Australian dollar.

The federal government signalled that it would seek partial wage indexation in the September wage hearing. Angered by this threat, a number of powerful unions - including coal miners and road transport workers - threatened to seek wage increases outside the arbitration system. Such action would have quickly destroyed the Accord. Rather than place its incomes policy at risk, the government then agreed to support full indexation at the September wage hearing, in exchange for a discount of 2.0% at the hearing in April, 1986. Deferred wage restraint placated financial markets. Also, the ACTU agreed to accept the future 2.0% discount on the condition that workers would be compensated with income tax cuts. Again, consent for incomes policy had been preserved by the use of fiscal policy.

A further reason for the success of the Accord was the record of the government in establishing supporting mechanisms. Some of these fell outside the narrow field of industrial relations, in areas such as industrial legislation, occupational health and safety, equal employment opportunity, and employment stimulation and creation programmes. Of more direct significance were the establishment of the Prices Surveillance Authority in March, 1984, and the extension of controls over non-wage incomes. These measures not only fulfilled promises made to the union movement in February, 1983, but helped to turn the Accord into a comprehensive prices and incomes policy, rather than just a wages policy.

One final element in the Accord merits discussion. This is the extension of consultative mechanisms to draw unions, employers and other interest groups into the process of political decision making and economic planning. While 'open government' has had complex ramifications throughout the federal bureaucracy, there are three new institutions of special importance. First is the Economic Planning

113

Advisory Council (EPAC), which was established after the 'summit,' and which is chaired by the Prime Minister, and made up of the Federal Treasurer and Minister for Industrial Relations, four ACTU nominees, five business nominees, three state premiers, and representatives of local government, welfare and consumer groups. Second is the Advisory Committee on Prices and Incomes (ACPI) established in October of 1983 to advise upon implementing prices and incomes policy. This had eighteen members. It is chaired by the Minister for Industrial Relations, and includes the Treasurer and ministers from three states and the Northern Territory. In addition, there are six union nominees, and five representa- tives from the two rival employers' federations - the CAI and the Business Council of Australia. Third is the Australian Manufacturing Council (AMC) which has 28 members drawn from unions and employers in the main segments of manufacturing. Beneath the AMC there is a network of Industry Councils which deal with industry development in specific industries. Several of these bodies have conducted inquiries parallel to the Industries Assistance Commission (IAC), which reviews tariff protection.

Any assessment of these and the other consultative bodies established under the Accord, is made difficult by the complex nature of their functions, by their procedures, and by the short period most have been in operation. However, it is clear that relations with the existing federal bureaucracy have constrained a number of these bodies. Several of the industry councils, however, have been judged a success, as a result of which the Hancock Committee of Review endorsed proposals that they be more fully integrated into the industrial relations machinery of those industries that chose such arrangements.

CONCLUSION

Although there has not been (and cannot be) unequivocal proof of the Accord's success, it is generally acclaimed as an effective economic and social policy. It is thought to have assisted the economic recovery since 1983, led to a dramatic downturn in industrial conflict, and encouraged informed and orderly debate upon social and industrial development.

Despite this, it remains an unstable policy device, liable to break down under adverse economic and political circumstances. Events following the collapse of the Australian dollar in mid-1985 illustrated how easily the Australian Labour Party could lose union support if wage restraint was imposed in a generally buoyant economy. Generally, the Accord is imperilled by the continuous tension between union demands for an equity-based policy, and employer demands for economic responsiveness.

The success of the Accord is, perhaps, all the more remarkble when the circumstances of its adoption are compared with those in 1975 when indexation was introduced. Generally, wage indexation benefited from a depressed labour market, which disciplined unions into accepting tight central control over pay. In contrast, the Accord has been sustained during a period of employment growth, rising profitability, and rapid economic growth.

How is it possible to maintain an orderly incomes policy in such an economic situation? Perhaps the most important factor here is the priority given by the government to incomes policy in comparison with other branches of economic policy. Whereas the Fraser Liberal/National party government strained incomes policy by expecting it to support its monetary and fiscal strategies, the Hawke Labour government has used other economic and social policies to shore up its incomes policy.

One result of this is that the responsibility for incomes policy in the period 1983-85 is very different from that during the period 1976-81. In the first period, the Commission bore most of the responsibility for incomes policy administration - often in the context of adverse government action. Since 1983 the government - including the bureaucracy and the consultative machinery - have had a stronger role vis-a-vis the Commission. To simplify, the Accord is a government incomes policy, whereas wage indexation was a Commission incomes policy.

The authority of the government is the more remarkable given its weak constitutional powers. The absence of such direct power, however, might serve to remind of the need to negotiate incomes policy rather than impose it. The record of the Hawke government in the area of prices and incomes rests primarily upon its willingness to negotiate, both with the ACTU, with which it preserves a special relationship, and with employers.

A negotiated approach is not without its critics. Amongst these are leading opposition politicians, who condemn the Accord as capitulation to union power. Notice has been served that the fabric of the Accord - centralised wage fixation, supporting mechanisms, and consultative machinery - could fall victim to a swing against the Hawke Labour government. This may not signify the end of incomes policies, but perhaps that they would return to the custodianship of the Commission.

FOOTNOTES

1. Submissions to the Committee of Review into Industrial Relations Law and Systems (Department of Employment and Industrial Relations, Canberra, 1984).
2. McGuinness, P.P., The Case against the Arbitration Commission (Centre for Independent Studies, Sydney, 1985).
3. Hancock Committee, Report of the Committee of Review upon Australian Industrial Relations Law and Systems, Vol. II, (AGPS, Canberra, 1985).
4. Blandy, R., 'The Future of Australia's Industrial Relations System: A Summary and Comment,' Australian Bulletin of Labour, Supplement No. 5 (1984), sl - sl0.
5. Schott, K., Policy, Power and Order: The Persistence of Economic Problems in Capitalist States (Yale University Press, New Haven, 1984).
6. Plowman, D., Wage Indexation (Allen & Unwin, Sydney, 1981), pp. 98-99.
7. Plowman, D., 'Union Statistics: Scope and Limitations,' in Ford, B. and D. Plowman (eds.), Australian Unions (MacMillan, London, 1983), pp. 531-532.
8. Yerbury, D., 'Collective Negotiations, Wage Indexation and the Return to Arbitration, Some Institutional and Legal Developments during the Whitlam Era,' in Ford, G.W., J.M. Hearn and R.D. Lansbury (eds.) Australian Labour Relations Readings, 3rd edn. (MacMillan, London, 1980), pp. 468-471.
9. Statement of Accord by the Australian Labour Party and the Australian Council of Trade Unions Regarding Economic Policy (1983).
10. Scherer, P., 'The Goals of Incomes Policy,' in Hancock, K. (ed.), Incomes Policy in Australia (Harcourt Brace Jovanovitch, London, 1981).
11. Isaac, J.E., 'Penal Provisions Under Commonwealth Arbitration,' in Isaac, J.E. and G.W. Ford (eds.), Australian Labour Relations: Readings, 2nd edn. (Sun Books, Melbourne, 1971).

12. Hancock, K., 'The First Half-Century of Australian Wage Policy - Part I,' Journal of Industrial Relations (1979).

13. Phelps Brown, E.H., 'Industrial Relations and the Law: Lessons of Australian Experience,' Three Banks Review (March, 1971), p. 21.

14. Macarthy, P.G., 'Justice Higgins and the Harvester Judgement,' in Roe, J., (ed.), Social Policy in Australia (Cassell Australia, Sydney, 1976).

15. Hawke, R.J., 'The Commonwealth Arbitration Court - Legal Tribunal or Economic Legislature,' in Isaac, J.E. and G.W. Ford (eds.), Australian Labour Economics, 1st edn. (Sun Books, Melbourne, 1967).

16. Isaac, J.E., 'Wage Determination and Economic Policy,' Australian Economic Review, No. 3 (1977), pp. 16-24.

17. National Wage Case, Reasons for Decision, Print No. E9700 (1982).

18. Wedderburn, K.W. and W.T. Murphy, Labour Law and the Community Perspectives for the 1980s (Institute for Advanced Legal Studies, London, 1983).

19. Ss. 36 and 36A.

20. Ibid., s. 39(2).

21. Ibid., ss. 11A - 14.

22. Carboch, D., 'The Fall of the Bruce-Page Government,' in Mayer, H. (ed.), Studies in Australian Politics (Cheshire, Melbourne, 1958).

23. Plowman, Wage Indexation, pp. 137-138.

24. Conciliation and Arbitration Act, s. 40(1) (c).

25. Staples, J.F., 'Uniformity and Diversity in Industrial Relations,' Journal of Industrial Relations (1980).

26. Hancock Committee, Report, pp. 103-122.

27. Niewenhuysen, J., 'The South Australian Industrial Commission and the Demise of Wage Indexation,' Journal of Industrial Relations (1981), pp. 508-516.

28. Isaac, 'Penal Provisions,' pp. 45-465.

29. d'Alpuget, B., Mediator, A Biography of Sir Richard Kerby (Melbourne University Press, Melbourne, 1977) pp. 199-237; Dabscheck, B., Arbitrator at Work: Sir William Raymond Kelly and the Regulation of Australian Industrial Relations (Allen & Unwin, Sydney, 1983), pp. 116-158.

30. Cupper, L., 'Legalism in the Australian Conciliation and Arbitration Commission: The Gradual Transition,' Journal of Industrial Relations (1976).

31. National Wage Case, Reasons for Decision (1982), Print No. E9700.

32. Crean, S. & M. Rimmer, 'Unions and Industrial Relations Reform,' in Blandy, R. and J.R. Niland (eds.) Alternatives to the Present Arbitration System (Allen and Unwin, Sydney, 1985).

33. Plowman, Wage Indexation, p. 6.

34. Hughes, B., Exit Full Employment (Angus & Robertson, Sydney, 1980), pp. 69-84.

35. Ibid., pp. 162-168.

36. Cameron, C., Unions in Crisis (Hill of Content, Melbourne, 1982), pp. 244-274.

37. Yerbury, 'Collective Negotiations,' pp. 470-471.

38. National Wage Case, Wage Fixation Principles Case (1978).

39. National Wage Case, Reasons for Decision (1979), Print No. E267.

40. National Wage Case, Reasons for Decision (1981), Print No. E5000.

41. Hancock Committee, Report, p. 161.

42. Phipps, A.J., 'The Impact of Wage Indexation on Wage Inflation in Australia 1975-1980,' Australian Economic Review (1982).

43. Sheehan, P., 'Wages Policy and the Economy in the Seventies and Beyond,' in Hancock, Incomes Policy, p. 165.

44. Commonwealth Treasurer, Budget Statement 1982-83 (AGPS, Canberra, 1982).

45. Commonwealth Government, Submission to the National Wage Case, February-March, 1985 (AGPS, Canberra, 1985).

46. Dawkins, P. and R. Blandy, 'Labour Costs and the Future of the Accord,' paper presented to the 14th Conference of Economists at the University of New South Wales (13-17 May, 1985), p. 30.

REFERENCES

ALP/ACTU, Statement of Accord by the Australian Labor Party and the Australian Council of Trade Unions regarding Economic Policy (1983).

Blandy, R., 'The Future of Australia's Industrial Relations System: A Summary and Comment,' Australian Bulletin of Labour, Supplement No. 5 (1984).

Cameron, C., Unions in Crisis, (Hill of Content, Melbourne, 1982).

Committee of Review upon Australian Industrial Relations Law and Systems (Hancock Committee),

Report, Vol. II (Australian Government Printing Service, Canberra, 1985).

Commonwealth Government, Submission to the National Wage Case, February-March, 1985 (Australian Government Printing Service, Canberra, 1985).

Commonwealth Treasurer, Budget Statement, 1982-83 (Australian Government Printing Service, Canberra, 1982).

Crean, S. & Rimmer, M., 'Unions and Industrial Relations Reform,' in Blandy, R. and Niland, J.R. (eds.), Alternatives to the Present Arbitration System (Allen & Unwin, Sydney, 1985).

Cupper, L., 'Legalism in the Australian Conciliation and Arbitration Commission: The Gradual Transition,' Journal of Industrial Relations (1976).

Dabscheck, B., Arbitrator at Work: Sir William Raymond Kelly and the Regulation of Australian Industrial Relations (Allen & Unwin, Sydney, 1983).

d'Alpuget, B., Mediator, A Biography of Sir Richard Kirby (Melbourne University Press, Melbourne, 1977).

Dawkins, P. & Blandy, R., 'Labour Costs and the Future of the Accord,' Paper presented to the 14th Conference of Economists at the University of New South Wales, 13th-17th May, 1985.

Department of Employment and Industrial Relations, Submissions to the Committee of Review into Industrial Relations Law and Systems (Australian Government Printing Service, Canberra, 1984).

Ford, B. and Plowman, D. (eds.), Australian Unions (MacMillan, Sydney, 1983).

Ford, G.W., J.M. Hearn and R.D. Lansbury (eds.), Australian Labour Relations: Readings, Third Edition (MacMillan, Sydney, 1980).

Hancock, K. 'The First Half-Century of Australian Wage Policy - Part I,' Journal of Industrial Relations (1979).

Hancock, K. (ed.), Incomes Policy in Australia (Harcourt Brace Jovanovich, London, 1981).

Hughes, B., Exit Full Employment (Angus & Robertson, Sydney, 1980).

Isaac, J.E. & Ford, G.W. (eds.), Australian Labour Relations, Readings, First and Second Edition, (Sun Books, Melbourne, 1967 and 1971).

Isaac, J.E., 'Wage Determination and Economic Policy,' Australian Economic Review, No. 3 (1977), pp. 16-24.

McGuinness, P.P., The Case against the Arbitration Commission, (Centre for Independent Studies,

Sydney, 1985).

Mayer, H. (ed.), Studies in Australian Politics
(Cheshire, Melbourne, 1958).

National Wage Case, Reasons for Decision, Print No.
E 267 (1979).

National Wage Case, Reasons for Decision, Print No.
E 5000 (1981).

National Wage Case, Reasons for Decision, Print No.
E 9700 (1982).

Niewenhuysen, J., 'The South Australian Industrial
Commission and the Demise of Wage Indexation,'
Journal of Industrial Relations (1981).

Phelps Brown, E.H., 'Industrial Relations and the
Law: Lessons of Australian Experience,' Three
Banks Review (1971).

Phipps, A.J., 'The Impact of Wage Indexation on Wage
Inflation in Australia: 1975-1980,' Australian
Economic Review (1982).

Plowman, D., Wage Indexation (Allen & Unwin, Sydney,
1981).

Roe, J. (ed.), Social Policy in Australia (Cassell
Australia, Sydney, 1976).

Schott, K., Policy, Power and Order: The Persistence
of Economic Problems in Capitalist States (Yale
University Press, New Haven, Conn., 1984).

Staples, J.F., 'Uniformity and Diversity in Industrial Relations,' Journal of Industrial Relations (1980).

Wedderburn, K.W. & Murphy, W.T., Labour Law and the
Community, Perspectives for the 1980s (Institute of Advanced Legal Studies, London,' 1983).

Chapter Four

CANADA: THE PERFECT ENVIRONMENT?

Beth Bilson

INTRODUCTION

The experience of post-war Canada in the battle
against inflation bears, of course, a resemblance to
that of other industrialised nations. There are,
however, certain characteristics peculiar to the
Canadian economic and political scene which must be
borne in mind in order to understand that battle in
its Canadian manifestation.

In her most important economic relationship,
Canada experiences more than the ordinary external
influence which every nation must acknowledge as a
potent factor in its development. She plays mouse
to the United States elephant, a role which produces
extraordinarily powerful forces in every aspect of
Canadian life. Historical preoccupations with
tariffs, with transportation and with alternative
sources of investment attest to this.

Of considerable significance for our purposes
here is the influence the United States has on
Canadian industrial relations and wage patterns.[1]
This impact is felt, not only because of the
sensitivity of Canadian wages to American economic
trends, but also because of the close links between
American trade unions and their Canadian counterparts, many of which are 'branch plants' of American
international unions. Though the 1960s and 1970s
saw the growth of some large Canadian unions,
particularly in the public sector, the fate of
organised workers in Canada is still to a large
degree entangled with the activities of trade unions
with headquarters in the United States.

There are two other characteristics of the
Canadian labour movement which deserve mention here.
The first is the high degree to which bargaining is
decentralised, with virtually all bargaining being

done at the local level. Exceptions to local bargaining occur mainly in the public sector, where bargaining may be carried on at a province-wide or even nation-wide basis. The decentralised nature of industrial relations has had a significant impact on the kind of response which the labour movement has made to efforts to moderate wage increases.

Relative to trade unions in countries like Great Britain, the Canadian labour movement has little overt political power. The formal political alliance of unions in Canada is with the New Democratic party, a social democratic party which has achieved little representation in the national Parliament, though it has on occasion formed provincial governments in western Canada. Association with the party has not succeeded in giving organised labour access to the levers of power, partly because political activity is largely carried out through constituency organisations rather than through trade unions as such. Furthermore, there is a strong element of western agricultural populism in the New Democratic party which makes it less single-mindedly labour-oriented than is the case with the British Labour party.

All Canadian economic and industrial activity must be seen in the context of the distinctive constitutional context of the country. In the federal system of Canada, the two levels of government, federal and provincial, derive their authority from the Constitution Act, 1982; this statute embodies the scheme for division of power between the two levels of government which was originally laid out in the British North America Act of 1867.[2] The scheme takes the form of a list of powers over which each level of government has authority.[3] In theory the division is not a hierarchical one; each government is sovereign while acting within its own sphere.

The nineteenth century division of powers has proved difficult to adapt to twentieth century conditions. Power to legislate concerning labour matters, for example, was held to belong to the provinces as part of their jurisdiction over 'property and civil rights,' while economic policy for the nation as a whole has been seen as falling under such federal heads of power as 'the public debt and property,' 'the regulation of trade and commerce,' and the so-called 'residuary power,' which gives the federal government power over 'such classes of Subjects as are expressly excepted in the Enumeration of the Classes of Subjects by this act assigned exclusively to the Legislatures of the Provinces.'[1]

Conflicts arising from the inevitable overlaps in these areas of influence may be dealt with either by the political process of federal-provincial agreement, by which powers may, in effect, be shared or assigned, or by means of reference of the issue to the courts. Both of these methods have had some relevance to incomes policies at various times.

A final constitutional characteristic which is of some significance is the presence in the Constitution Act of an entrenched Charter of Rights and Freedoms, formulated in 1982. Though the course of this Charter has not yet been firmly set, particularly in relation to matters concerning labour, it is already plain that the legitimacy of incomes policies, most clearly those which purport directly to regulate collective bargaining, will be evaluated in the light of the rights and freedom articulated in the Charter.

INCOME POLICIES IN THE POST-WAR PERIOD

From Wartime to the Sixties

Like other countries, Canada made attempts to control its economy directly during the Second World War, attempts which included a wage stabilisation policy instituted in 1941 to deal with the upward pressure on wages caused by the shortage of labour. National and regional War Labour Boards administered a scheme of wage limits which, along with other factors, appear to have slowed the rate of increase in basic wage rates from 18.2% in 1941-43 to 6.1% in 1943-45.[4]

The economy of Canada in the post-war period, like that in other industrialised nations, has generally been characterised by a gradual upward shift in the inflation rate. A comparison with the pre-war part of the century shows that at several points before the war, prices and wages fell, and thus the long-term pattern was relatively stable. Since the war, however, the trend has been almost continuously upward.[5]

For some time, this could be explained as part of the post-war recovery process, though economic dislocation had clearly not been as severe in Canada as in Europe. The problem of the 1950s appeared to be, not inflation, but recession; even the expansionary economy of the early 1960s produced an inflation rate which was only about 1.7%.[6]

The second half of the decade presented a somewhat different picture, however, with an average inflation rate of 4.1% between 1966 and 1969.[7] In 1968 and 1969, as wage rates climbed at an unprecedented 8% annually, and as the inflationary pressures exerted on the United States economy by the Vietnam conflict occasioned more alarm in Canada, government intervention, hitherto viewed as an extraordinary step to be reserved for crises such as depression and war, was increasingly a subject of discussion.[8] The government first embarked on a programme of weak monetary and fiscal measures, but these failed to have any significant effect.[9]

The Organisation for Economic Co-operation and Development enquired in its Economic Survey of 1968 why Canada had not attempted to institute an incomes policy.[10] Partly in response to this suggestion, the government established an inter-departmental committee of senior public servants to explore avenues for dealing with inflation. In addition, talks were held with representatives of provincial governments, and in September of 1968 Prime Minister Pierre Trudeau held informal meetings separately with senior trade union leaders and spokemen for associations of employers.[11]

The Prices and Incomes Commission

These discussions led to the presentation of a White Paper in December of 1968;[12] the document suggested that fiscal and monetary policy alone had not proved effective in defeating inflation and proposed the creation of a Prices and Incomes Commission which would explore possibilities for future policy.

As talks with the provinces, labour and business continued, the Prices and Incomes Commission was established in June of 1969; it survived until 31 August, 1972. The Commission was given two major tasks, the first being 'to inquire into and report upon the causes, processes and consequences of inflation,' the other 'to inform those making current price and income decisions, the general public and the government on how price stability may best be achieved.'[13]

The Commission was not, however, given any executive powers; it was thought that any concrete action would result from whatever sort of agreement emerged from the multi-party discussions. Nonetheless, the new body soon did succumb to pressures on it to move forward as the instrument of whatever

124

policy was to be adopted. Discussions moved quite rapidly towards some policy which would be more active, albeit voluntary, through the summer of 1969; the rapidity with which the Commission proceeded to devise proposals, along with suspicion of government bona fides because of cuts in public employment, finally alarmed the trade union representatives involved into declaring that they would not support the proposals being made.[14]

The defection of the trade unions made it appear that any idea of voluntary restraint was doomed, but the Commission pressed on with its attempt to formulate some programme of action. This took the form of the National Conference on Price Stability held in February of 1970, at which more than 250 persons, all senior representatives of a wide range of industrial sectors, were present.

Officials of the Commission had carefully prepared the ground for the conference by prior discussion with the participants; thus the agenda for the conference consisted of carefully-orchestrated discussion, by sectoral groups, of specific proposals. Those present were bluntly told that something had to be done and that it was no good pointing the finger at labour[15] - an interesting example of official rejection of cost-push theory.

In the hot glare of publicity, the participants in the conference agreed that business firms would ensure that price increases stayed below cost increases, and would provide the Prices and Incomes Commission with information for monitoring the agreement. All eleven Canadian governments subsequently agreed to apply the criteria to their own pricing policy.

The Commission seems to have been fairly successful at communicating a sense of urgency to the subscribers to the agreement; the incidence of compliance with the criteria agreed on at the conference remained high throughout 1970.

In June, the Prices and Incomes Commission called upon the trade unions to follow the example of industry, and to adopt a programme of voluntary restraint, limiting wage increases in the first year to 6%, and eschewing catch-up agreements; excessive wage increases would be reported to the federal government.

Though there was some interest in this effort - the Saskatchewan government refused certain contracts to construction firms whose workers made large wage demands - the intransigence of union hostility, and the abstention of some provinces, notably Ontario, from the scheme, prevented it from having any uniform effect. The Prices and Incomes Commission anxiously monitored wage settlements, and reported on some of them.

The targets may have had some effect on the non-unionised sector, but there was no discernible impact on collective bargaining.[16] This made it impossible to convince business leaders to prolong their efforts at price restraint beyond the end of 1970, and this aspect of the anti-inflation scheme floundered. The Prices and Incomes Commission thereafter increased its attention to the analytical task it had been given, and produced a number of studies and reports.[16] The final conclusions of the commission were published in a report of August, 1972, entitled 'Inflation, Unemployment and Incomes Policy.'[1] The report stated that inflationary pressures were likely to continue in Canada for the foreseeable future, and that should these escalate, 'a prices and incomes policy carefully integrated into general national and international economic policy is presently the best available instrument for achieving price stability while maintaining expanding employment opportunities.'[17] The Commission further concluded that any such policy to be successful would require a high degree of public support, as well as active participation by principal decision-makers in the economy, including business, labour and provincial governments, and that any worthwhile policy would have to be embodied in legislation.[18]

It may be said at this point that the insights offered by the Prices and Incomes Commission in this 1972 report have stood up remarkably well through subsequent periods of policy. In particular, the problem of reconciling the need for consensus with the need for coercion has been a continuing one, and one which remains baffling to any policy-maker contemplating a formal incomes policy.

The Commission's work was not completely forgotten. The national Conservative party advocated a comprehensive scheme of wage and price controls as part of its platform in the election campaign of 1974. The Liberal government, however, would not commit itself to such measures, recognising, perhaps, the political difficulties attendant on an anti-inflation programme.

Meanwhile, a variety of factors, including initiatives taken by the government to stimulate the economy, caused the inflation rate to accelerate

sharply through 1974; even a country as well-placed
as Canada to cope with international goods and oil
supply shocks was not immune to the impact of these
events.

The government did not initially think that
wage and price controls would be useful, as a large
proportion of Canada's inflation was 'imported.'[19] Nonetheless, as inflation worsened
in 1974, the government created an Ad Hoc Committee
of Senior Officials whose task was to initiate
renewed informal discussion with constituent groups
in the economy about possible solutions to the
problem of inflation.

The budget speech in November of 1974 sounded a
slightly new note, indicating that the major sources
of inflation were now domestic. In spite of this,
there was little enthusiasm for allowing the
'consensus-building' exercise which was going on
informally to proceed to a control programme, though
that was being discussed by economic mandarins.[20]

Discussions, including talks between the
Minister of Labour and trade union representatives,
continued through the spring of 1975; fairly
concrete proposals were apparently under consideration. The consensus notion received a severe
setback in May of 1975, when the Canadian Labour
Congress rejected restraint of the kind so far
discussed; that body called for more wide-spread
structural reform - housing measures, rent controls,
negative income tax for low-income workers and so on
- as a quid pro quo for any restraint
programme.[21]

Full-Scale Controls: The Anti-Inflation Programme
Though discussion had largely concerned voluntary
restraints, the possiblility of a more comprehensive
system of controls was mentioned occasionally.
Certainly the Minister of Finance in his budget
speech of June, 1975 made it clear that statutory
controls was one option which had been considered by
his department, though he also stated that the idea
had been shelved.[22] The Prime Minister also
publicly repudiated the idea of controls on the
grounds that experience in Britain and the United
States showed that 'when you take controls off you
begin more or less where you were before.'[23]

Still, a contingency plan for controls was
being formulated in the summer of 1975,[24] and
the Ad Hoc Committee of Senior Officials was
instructed in late September to prepare a plan for

mandatory controls, which were thought by someone,
if not the Prime Minister, to have become necessary
to slow inflation.[25]

In any event, on 13 October, 1975, on the
Thanksgiving weekend, Prime Minister Trudeau made a
televised address outlining a detailed plan for wage
and price restraint, 'the heaviest imposed on Canada
since the Second World War.' The Anti-Inflation
Programme thus introduced was presented, however,
not as an end in itself, but as a first step towards
a total reconstruction of an economy which had gone
beyond the point where short-term tinkering would be
of any value,[26] a vision not unlike that represented by the British National Plan of 1964. As the
Prime Minister expressed it, 'In this struggle, we
must accomplish nothing less than a wrenching
adjustment of our expectations - an adjustment of
our national life-style to our means.'[27] Shock
and outrage were expressed at the institution of the
comprehensive scheme of controls, at least by the
labour movement, though such expressions of surprise
were perhaps disingenuous. What seems in retrospect
to have been an inexorable progress by the government in the direction of controls should perhaps
have been anticipated by everyone who had followed
the course of government discussions; especially
striking was the consistency in the composition and
sentiment of the group of senior public officials
who had husbanded the idea of restraint since the
demise of the Price and Incomes Commission.

The White Paper[28] which introduced
discussion of anti-inflationary strategy stressed
that inflation must be attacked on a number of
fronts: fiscal and monetary measures; government
expenditure limits; social programmes aimed at food,
housing, energy, business activity and industrial
relations; and a prices and incomes policy establishing guidelines for 'responsible social behavior
in determining prices and incomes.'

The prices and incomes portion of this was
embodied in the Anti-Inflation Act, which was passed
on 3 December. Price and wage guidelines were set
for a period of three years at 8%, 6% and 4%, with
some allowance for productivity and past experience.
The emphasis in the White Paper was on the government's hope for voluntary compliance and the
intention to keep reporting and surveillance to a
minimum. The legislation acknowledged, however,
that statutory sanctions might prove necessary in
the event that co-operation was not forthcoming.

The combination of voluntariness with statutory

sanctions was reflected in the nature of the mechanisms which were chosen to implement the policy. To the Anti-Inflation Board was given the task of educating and guiding the Canadian public to cheerful compliance with the guidelines set out in the statute and the word 'cheerful' is perhaps not inapt, given the strong indentification in the public mind of the Board with its jovial Chairman, M. Jean-Luc Pepin. Though it was originally envisioned that this would be a matter of concentrating on large or important wage settlements or price changes, which would have the effect of setting the pattern that others would follow, the Board ultimately found itself - with a staff which numbered 917 at its peak - involved in the complicated task of investigating and comparing virtually every wage and price rise in the country.

Two important features of the Board's activity may be mentioned here, at the risk of oversimplifying what was obviously an enormously complex process. The first is the seriousness with which the Board took its responsibility of public education; throughout the control period, members of the Board and government politicians appeared before public gatherings in all parts of the country to spread the gospel of the struggle against inflation. The second feature, which almost goes without saying, was the degree of discretion exercised by the Board and its agents in applying the guidelines to specific situations.

The Anti-Inflation Administrator, on the other hand, was armed with extensive statutory powers, including the power to order repayment of individual wage and price increases which had already been made, and to exact a penalty for infractions of the guidelines.

Appeal from decisions of the Administrator lay to an Anti-Inflation Appeal Tribunal, and then to the Federal Court of Appeal, or in some circumstances to the federal Cabinet.

The scale of authority to enforce the Anti-Inflation Act which was confided to the tiny staff of the Office of the Administrator is worthy of special notice as a distinctive characteristic of the Canadian programme. It is perhaps one of the more startling features of this period that there was relatively little outcry at the time, and relatively little attention has been paid since, to the large amount of power wielded by these five or six little-known officials.

It was hoped that these extraordinary sanctions

would have to be used only sparingly, and this seems to have been the case. The possibility - and in some cases the actual imposition - of rollbacks and fines which could be in the hundreds of thousands of dollars seems to have had a sobering effect on the employers on whom the Anti-Inflation Board was trying to exercise its powers of persuasion, and to have been almost as effective by its existence as by its use.

The institution of a comprehensive national programme of wage and price controls of this kind created a serious constitutional problem for the Canadian government; it was not in a position simply to impose uniform economic policies covering all groups across the country. As one example, provincial government employees clearly did not fall within the range of federal government jurisdiction. The Act therefore provided that provincial governments could either give their assent to the national programme, or they could devise their own. It was hoped that none would choose to reject the idea of restraint altogether; in the event eight provinces placed themselves under the umbrella of the Anti-Inflation Act. The provinces of Saskatchewan and Quebec elected to establish their own mechanisms for dealing with their employees, though the latter did defect altogether following the election of the Parti Quebecois government after about one year.[29]

Furthermore, there was some doubt as to whether Ottawa had the power to legislate so generally on matters of economic policy. It had long been established that labour and industrial relations fell under the jurisdiction of the provinces and the anti-inflation legislation clearly affected those matters. The Attorney-General of Canada therefore agreed to refer to the Supreme Court of Canada the question of whether Parliament had the constitutional authority to pass the Anti-Inflation Act; representatives of several trade unions, as well as five provincial governments, intervened in the case to ensure that their interests would be considered.

The Court declared the legislation valid,[30] not as an exercise of the federal government's jurisdiction over any of the subjects enumerated in s.91 of the BNA. Act, but under the general clause which empowered the Canadian government 'to make Laws for the Peace, Order and good government of Canada.' The application of this phrase had been carefully confined over the preceding century by judicial interpretation, or the division of powers would have been meaningless. This caution was reflected in the judgment of the Court on the Anti-Inflation Reference. The approval of the Act was stated in the opinion of the Chief Justice as based on a conclusion that inflation was 'an evil of nation-wide proportions'[31] justifying Parliament's invocation of its general power. Another of the judges was even more cautious, stating that the passage of the Anti-Inflation Act had been necessitated by circumstances tantamount to a 'national emergency.'[32]

However well all this accorded with traditions of constitutional interpretation, the fact that legitimacy for the Act was grounded in a finding that economic circumstances were sufficiently calamitous to justify federal action caused at least one critic to complain that the terms of the decision doomed any outlook for a coherent national economic policy.[33]

The Anti-Inflation Programme was initially quite popular. A poll taken in November of 1975 showed 62% of the Canadian population to favour the controls; 54% favoured wage controls, while 70% supported price controls.[34] The organised labour movement stated its hostility from the outset, supported by the New Democratic party, which commenced a campaign to demonstrate that the controls would have a greater impact on wages than on prices.[35] Argument over whether the price controls were mere window-dressing continued throughout the life of the programme.

As was the experience in other countries, public enthusiasm for the programme cooled as time went on. The labour movement continued to object to controls and mounted a Day of Protest on the first anniversary, 14 October, 1976, on which over 800,000 workers absented themselves from their jobs.[36]

The Day of Protest gesture was really the zenith of labour action against the control programme, after a year in which a significant amount of effort had been put into educating Canadian workers about the effects of controls, and the largest national labour organisation, the Canadian Labour Congress, had declared in the strongest terms its intention to attempt to defeat the programme - a determination evident in the manifesto drawn up by the Congress,[37] and in its decision to intervene in the reference of the Act to the Supreme Court of Canada.

There is no doubt that the Day of Protest and other lesser demonstrations were a significant expression by union members of discontent with the control programme. Yet the Day of Protest was far from being a general strike, and in general, the posture of the Canadian public, union members included, was one of acquiescence or resignation rather than militant hostility.

The Act provided for an expiry date of 31 December, 1978, and by early 1977, policy-makers were putting their minds to the question of how to move out of the programme without experiencing an inflation 'explosion.' As the prospect of decontrol came closer, and activity in the programme showed no sign of letting up, consensus discussions similar to those which had taken place in 1974-75 were revived in early 1978. Several meetings were held which revealed a consensus of business and labour for bringing controls to an end and that a 'lights out' approach was preferred by them.[38]

The government's commitment to specific proposals for phased decontrol caused the talks to break down, and delayed the winding-down of the Anti-Inflation Programme until April of 1978. Part of the decontrol process was to turn over the monitoring function to the Economic Council of Canada, which established the Centre for the Study of Inflation and Productivity in June; the task of the Centre was to monitor wages and prices in the period after the controls expired at the end of the year, and to make policy recommendations to the government.

The Centre was still in its cradle when it was abolished in March of 1979, to be replaced by a National Council on Inflation attached to the Department of Finance, which was supposedly given more rigorous monitoring powers - a moot point, as the Council itself was eradicated by a new Progressive Conservative government in May.

The Post-Control Period

The concern over the wage and price explosion which might occur as the controls were lifted proved, in Canada's case, to be unwarranted. Though prices and wages did move upward again, there appears not to have been any catching up with the rate of inflation which might have been projected before the Anti-Inflation Programme.[40]

There are a number of possible explanations for this. Though the controls had been criticised in some quarters, the majority of Canadians had regarded them as necessary. The Canadian control programme was implemented in circumstances which would not have amounted to an inflation crisis elsewhere, but the perception of Canadians was of course influenced by their own experience. That the Supreme Court of Canada built a rationale of 'national emergency' in support of the Anti-Inflation Act on the foundation of a wage inflation rate of 13.2%[41] in 1974 and 14.2%[42] in 1975, at a time when British wages were rising at 20-30% may seem slightly odd, but there was widespread and genuine concern about this trend, especially with the noticeable food and petroleum price increases of 1973.

One striking response to the price rises of the early 1970s in Canada was the increased popularity of wage settlements containing cost of living allowance (COLA) clauses, a form of indexing provision which initially produced a significant trend to longer agreements. Both the number and the length of agreement with COLA clauses began to decline in the middle of the decade, signifying perhaps a loss of faith in the protection provided by indexation.[43] This pattern of increase and decline in the popularity of COLA clauses seems to have been independent of the impact of the controls.

The experience with COLA clauses lends some support to the notion that inflationary wage pressures arose as a one-to-one response to inflationary experience.[44] There was, of course, considerable controversy over whether the controls programme was successful in mitigating such inflationary pressure. The argument was made that these interventionist measures were adopted as a result of a stubborn adherence by the federal government to the prediction that inflation would continue to rise, when other forecasts predicted a decline in the inflation rate.[45]

There was support, however, for the government's claims that the programme had some effect in ratcheting down wage rates over its life. Federal government data showed the average annual compound increase in base rates over the life of agreements dropping from 17.2% in 1975, to 10.2% in 1976, to 7.7% in 1977.[46] The moderation of rates calculated per person employed was not quite so dramatic, but still showed a steady decline - 14.7% to 13.2% to 8.9%.[47]

Some commentators on the programme have suggested that the limits imposed by the controls were not ambitious enough,[48] or comprehensive enough

- they left out farm incomes, for example[49] - but that they had, in their own terms, been a success. One study - in what may be the most sterotypically Canadian of all such conclusions - included this summation:

> The program was modest and apparently made a modest contribution to reducing the rate of inflation, and also served the useful purpose of allowing politicians to be <u>seen</u> to be doing something about inflation. We could have done far worse.[50]

Another examination of the period concluded more confidently that the program had had a 'significant' indirect effect in depressing wage rates, and that, furthermore, this effect had increased during the life of the controls.[51] One subsequent commentator, using comparisons with Canada's experience has suggested that in the early 1980s the programme administered by the Anti-Inflation Board had a measurable impact in heading off a major recession in the late 1970s.[52]

There was much controversy over whether the controls bit into prices as firmly as they did into wages.[53] The government and the officials of the Anti-Inflation Board went to great lengths to present the policy as one which attacked price inflation as well as wages; the labour movement maintained with some vehemence that the price control apparatus was superficial and ineffective. Recent evidence suggests that the programme did have a moderating effect on prices;[54] if this is the case, it may have helped to create a psychological environment which made mushrooming demands on the cessation of controls less likely.

The acceptance of controls and the absence of a wage explosion on their removal may in part be explained by the fact that, even when the controls were having their most pronounced effect, real wages for the Canadian worker continued to climb - as the apologists for the policy had predicted.[55] In comparison with the experience in Britain, where real wages suffered declines as well as advances, the more regular upward Canadian trend gave defenders of the policy useful support.

Controls in the Public Sector
For one sector of Canadian workers, the bite of wage controls went somewhat deeper, according to their

Canada: The Perfect Environment?

own intuition and according to more objective
students of the controls.[56] The added rigour of
the programme as it affected the nation's public
employees may have owed something to goverment
determination to set an example of restraint in
their own domain, and to the uniformity in adhering
to the guidelines which could be required of
government departments and agencies. It probably
could not be attributed to the docility of the
Canadian unions representing these workers, which
were, in fact, the focus of what sustained
opposition there was to the restraint programme.

As in many industrialised countries, the 1980s
have been for Canada a period of economic anxiety
and recession, characterised by government retrenchment and eventual resort to neoclassical economic
ideas, the latter illustrated most forcefully in the
policies of the Social Credit government of British
Columbia, and in the election of a Conservative
federal government in September of 1984 which had
campaigned on a platform of free-market conservatism.

Voluntarism and Public Sector Restraint in the 1980s
Perhaps in keeping with its rationalisation as a
crisis-management instrument in the 1970s, the
concept of formal controls was not resuscitated in
the first half of the 1980s. Indeed in 1982,
Liberal Prime Minister Trudeau ringingly rejected
the idea of a new round of controls, and sounded the
call for voluntarism:

> Controls would declare, with the force of law,
> that Canadians cannot trust Canadians...To
> choose to fight inflation, as a free people
> acting together - that is the course we
> chose.[57]

Nonetheless, if general inflation was not seen
as the high profile problem of the 1980s, unre-
strained government spending was. Though the only
wage controls of the 1980s appeared in the form of
threatened unemployment and economic recession in
the private sector, they still commonly took a more
direct form for public sector workers.

From 1982, the federal government took specific
action to place limits on the compensation received
by workers in the public sector, through the '6 and
5' legislation[58] which provided that public
employees would be limited to wage increases of 6%

135

in the first year after the passage of the statute, and 5% the year following that.[59] The mechanism for achieving this was to extend the life of existing collective agreements by two years, though collective bargaining might take place to alter terms and conditions of employment other than wages.[60]

A number of provincial governments followed the example set by the Canadian government, in some cases by the use of the same device of extending the life of agreements.[61] Related legislation in some provinces, most notably British Columbia, gave governments expanded rights to dismiss or permanently lay off workers.[62]

This period of legislative activity in Canada was not overtly directed at inflation and was classified as one of voluntarism by governments, and by the public generally; but for Canadian public sector workers it represented an even more drastic intervention in the determination of their terms of employment than the 1975-78 controls. This was partly because the statutes passed in this period abandoned all pretense of deference to the collective bargaining process and directly regulated the length and terms of collective agreements; it is debatable, perhaps, whether this was a dramatic change in substance, as the rollback powers of the earlier anti-inflation machinery had essentially the same effect.

It is perhaps a more crucial feature of the 1980s legislation that public sector workers were singled out for direct restraint, and that a comprehensive call for sacrifice was not issued on this occasion.

The Charter Challenge

The public workers of the 1980s had one new weapon, whose strength had yet to be tried. This was the Canadian Charter of Rights and Freedoms which had emerged as the most prominent aspect of a package of constitutional changes made in 1982.

The Charter was, at first reading, not a promising instrument for labour movement use in a challenge to restraint legislation. It made no explicit provision for the rights of workers or trade unions, and critics sympathetic to labour expressed the fear that, in fact, a number of the provisions of the Charter would prove incompatible with the collective aspirations of the trade union movement.

Canada: The Perfect Environment?

A number of trade unions, however, decided to mount an attack on the restraint legislation, arguing that the extension of collective agreements and the overriding of collective bargaining by legislators was an infringement of the right to strike and carry out other union activities which were implicit in the freedoms of assembly and association entrenched in the Charter. These challenges had varying degrees of success in the provincial courts;[63] at the time of writing, none of the cases which reached the Supreme Court of Canada had been decided, and the nation's highest court had yet to express its opinion on the issue.

A kind of parallel scrutiny of this 1980s restraint legislation in Canadian jurisdictions was conducted in 1985 by a deputation of the International Labour Organisation despatched to evaluate these statutes in the light of international labour conventions promoting freedom of association and the rights of labour organisations. Restraint legislation in the provinces of Newfoundland, Ontario, Alberta and British Columbia were declared to be incompatible with these international conventions. The avenues for correcting the conditions which provoked these judgments are far from evident, though it has been argued that it is potentially highly embarrassing for governments in a country which had indulged in a certain amount of self-congratulation for its progressive labour policies to be the object of such censure. Given the supply-side list to the policies of the governments in question, it may be that they think such embarrassment a small price to pay for setting their economies on the right course.

The intervention of the International Labour Organisation is nonetheless cause for interesting speculation about this particular form of incomes policy - or non-policy. It would be interesting to know whether formal controls of the kind established in the mid-1970s, under which collective bargaining continued, in theory, to flourish unimpeded would have been viewed the same way; or whether it is the choice of direct manipulation of the public sector collective bargaining system, combined with ostensible adherence to the principles of voluntarism, which led the international body to censure the restraint legislation.

The official '6 and 5' federal statutory policy ended in 1984, but Canadian governments have continued to insist on restraint in the public sector - by spending cutbacks, by layoffs of large

137

numbers of public workers, and by stating minimal
wage increases as a goal for public employers. The
climate of economic gloom and an alarming level of
unemployment in Canadian terms helped to sustain the
public acceptance of the apparent discrepancy
between government protestations of economic voluntarism combined with severe restraints on that large
segment of the economy over which these same governments have direct influence.

CONCLUSION

It has been suggested that the basic choice facing
Canada in the 1980s is between further formal wage
and price controls or ever-mounting unemployment;[64] the same authors comfortingly suggest
that Canada is peculiarly suited to centralised
programmes of the type implemented in the mid-1970s,
particularly if sensible monetary and fiscal
restraints are used as well.[65] There are
factors which can be cited as obstacles to achieving
the national consensus necessary as a basis for
voluntary restraints of the kind which can be
identified in some countries - the political disenfranchisement of the labour movement, differences
in economic influences and activities, the difficulty of rousing passionate commitment to a
political or economic programme - though consensus
may still be worth aiming for.[66] It must be
remembered, however, that the same factors make it
difficult for any individual or group to mount a
nationally-based opposition to any rational proposal for wage and price policy. This could offer
to Canadian governments the incentive to attempt
future episodes of formal controls; they may not
plan for wild success, but neither need they fear
great disaster.

FOOTNOTES

1. Smith, Douglas A., 'Wage Linkages between
Canada and the United States,' Industrial and Labor
Relations Review, vol. 29 (January, 1976), p. 258.
2. 30 & 31 Vict., ch. 3.
3. Ibid., ss. 91-92.
4. Chernick, Sidney E., 'Wage Controls in
Canada, 1940-1946,' in Wood, W.D. and Pradeep Kumar
(eds.), Canadian Perspectives on Wage Price Guidelines (Queen's University Industrial Relations
Centre, Kingston, Ont., 1976), pp. 168-174.

Canada: The Perfect Environment?

5.   Anti-Inflation Board, Inflation and Public
Policy (Minister of Supply and Services, Ottawa,
1979), p. 12.
6.   Carr, Jack, 'Wage and Price Controls:
Panacea for Inflation - Prescription for Disaster?'
in The Illusion of Wage and Price Control (The
Fraser Institute, Vancouver, 1976), p. 23.
7.   Ibid.
8.   Haythorne, George V., 'Prices and Incomes
Policy: The Canadian Experience, 1969-1972,' International Labour Review, vol. 103 (1973), p. 486.
9.   McKee, Arnold F., 'Wage-price Guidelines:
Canada's Approach,' in Wood and Kumar (eds.),
Canadian Perspectives, p. 232.
10.   Ibid.
11.   Haythorne, 'Prices and Incomes,' p. 488.
12.   Policies for Price Stability (Department
of Consumer and Corporate Affairs, Ottawa, 1968).
13.   Haythorne, 'Prices and Incomes,' p. 488.
14.   Ibid., p. 493.
15.   Interview with Mr. George Haythorne,
1979.
16.   Including an unpublished report outlining
a possible scheme of formal wage and price controls
which may have had some impact on subsequent policy
in the United States: see Haythorne, 'Prices and
Incomes,' p. 499.
17.   Ibid.
18.   Ibid.
19.   Anti-Inflation Board, Chronicles of the
AIB (Anti-Inflation Board, Ottawa, 1979), p. 20.
20.   Ibid., p. 23.
21.   Ibid., p. 27.
22.   Canada - House of Commons, Debates, vol.
VIII (14 October, 1975), p. 8214.
23.   Quoted in Ibid., p. 8374.
24.   Interview with Mr. T.K. Shoyama (Department of Finance - Canada), 1979.
25.   Anti-Inflation Board, Chronicles, p. 29.
26.   McLeod, T.H., 'Anti-Inflation Administration: The Setting,' (unpublished, 1979), p. 2.
27.   Ibid., p. 8.
28.   'Attack on Inflation: A Program of
National Action,' (Department of Finance, Ottawa,
October, 1975).
29.   Anti-Inflation Board, Chronicles, p. 41.
30.   Anti-Inflation Act Reference (1976), 9
N.R. 541.
31.   Ibid. p. 564.
32.   Ibid., p. 599.
33.   Weiler, Paul in 'Industrial Relations

after Wage and Price Controls Panel Discussion,'
Canadian Public Policy/Analyse de Politiques, vol. 4
(1978), p. 440.
    34. Anti-Inflation Board, Chronicles, p. 145.
    35. Ibid., p. 149.
    36. Staudohar, Paul, 'Effects of Wage and
Price Controls in Canada, 1975-78,' Relations
Industrielles/Industrial Relations, vol. 34 (1979),
p. 680.
    37. Canadian Labour Congress, 'Labour's Mani-
festo for Canada,' (Canadian Labour Congress,
Ottawa, 1976).
    38. Powis, Alfred, in Consultation and Con-
sensus: A New Era in Policy Formulation (Conference
Board in Canada, Ottawa, 1978), p. 29.
    39. Ostry, Sylvia, Report of the Centre for
the Study of Inflation and Productivity to the First
Minister's Conference (Economic Council of Canada,
Ottawa, November, 1978), p. 5.
    40. Barber, Clarence and John C.P. McCallum,
Controlling Inflation: Learning from Experience in
Canada, Europe and Japan (James Lorimer/Canadian
Institute for Economic Policy, Toronto, 1982), p.
22.
    41. Kumar, Pradeep, 'The Current Canadian Wage
Scene,' in Wood and Kumar, Canadian Perspectives, p.
293.
    42. Department of Finance Canada, Economic
Review (Department of Finance, Ottawa, April, 1978),
p. 53.
    43. Department of Finance Canada, Canada's
Recent Inflation Experience (Department of Finance,
Ottawa, 1978), p. 33.
    44. Ostry, Sylvia and Mahmood A. Zaidi, Labour
Economics in Canada, 3rd ed. (MacMillan, Toronto,
1979) p. 248.
    45. Walker, Michael, 'Are Wage and Price
Controls Working?' in Which Way Ahead? (The Fraser
Institute, Vancouver, 1977), p. 52.
    46. Department of Finance, Economic Review, p.
29.
    47. Department of Finance, Canada's Recent
Inflation, p. 52,
    48. Interview with Mr. Rob Douglas (Department
of Finance Canada), 1979.
    49. Interview with Mr. T.H. McLeod (AIA).
    50. Wilson, Thomas A. and Gregory V. Jump, The
Influence of the Anti-Inflation Program on Aggregate
Wages and Prices (Anti-Inflation Board, Ottawa,
1979), p. 43.
    51. Christofides, L.N. and D.A. Wilton, Wage

Controls in Canada (1976:3 - 1978:2): A Study of
Their Impact on Negotiated Base Wage Rates (Anti-
Inflation Board, Ottawa, 1979).
    52. McCallum, John, 'Two Cheers for the AIB,'
Canadian Public Policy/Analyse de Politiques vol. 12
(March, 1986), p. 142.
    53. See Maslove, Allan and Gene Swimmer, Wage
Controls in Canada 1975-1978: A Study of Public
Decision-Making (Institute for Research on Public
Policy, Montreal, 1980); Wilson, T.A. and G.V. Jump,
The Influence of the Anti-Inflation Program on Wages
and Prices: A Simulation Analysis (Anti-Inflation
Board, Ottawa, 1979).
    54. Barber and McCallum, Controlling Infla-
tion, p. 24.
    55. Finance Canada, Economic Review, p. 33.
    56. Auld, D.A.L., L.N. Christofides et al,
'The Impact of the Anti-Inflation Board on Negoti-
ated Wage Settlements,' Canadian Journal of Econo-
mics, vol. 12 (1979), p. 201; Christofides and
Wilton, Wage Controls, p. 83.
    57. Quoted in Thompson, Mark and Gene Swimmer
(eds.), Conflict or Compromise: The Future of Public
Sector Industrial Relations (Institute for Research
on Public Policy, Montreal, 1984), p. 425.
    58. Public Sector Compensation Restraint Act,
S.C. 1980-81-82-83, c. 122.
    59. Ibid., s. 2(3).
    60. Ibid., s. 7.
    61. E.g. Inflation Restraint Act, S.O., 1982,
c. 55.
    62. Thompson, Mark, 'Restraint and Labour
Relations: The Case of British Columbia,' Canadian
Public Policy/Analyse de Politiques vol. 11 (June,
1985), p. 171.
    63. Re Service Employees' International Union,
Local 204 and Broadway Manor Nursing Home (1983), 44
O.R. (2d) 392 (Ont. H.C.); Public Service Alliance
of Canada v. The Queen, [1984] 2 F.C. 889 (Fed. Ct.
App. Div.); Reference Re Public Service Employee
Relations Act, Labour Relations Act and Police
Officers Collective Bargaining Act, [1985] 2 W.W.R.
289 (Alta. C.A.); Retail, Wholesale and Department
Store Union v. Government of Saskatchewan, [1985] 5
W.W.R. 97 (Sask. C.A.).
    64. Barber andd McCallum, Controlling Infla-
tion, p. 109; McCallum 'Two Cheers,' p. 142.
    65. Ibid., Chapters 2 and 6.
    66. Barber, Clarence, 'Jobs, Jobs: Specific
Proposals,' Policy Options, (April, 1986), p. 3.

Canada: The Perfect Environment?

REFERENCES

Anti-Inflation Board, Chronicles of the AIB (Anti-
    Inflation Board, Ottawa, 1979).
Anti-Inflation Board, Inflation and Public Policy
    (Anti-Inflation Board, Ottawa, 1979).
Auld, D.A.L., L.N. Christofides et al, 'The Impact
    of the Anti-Inflation Board on Negotiated Wage
    Settlements,' Canadian Journal of Economics,
    vol. 12 (1979) p. 261.
Barber, Clarence and John C.P. McCallum, Controlling
    Inflation: Learning from Experience in Canada,
    Europe and Japan (James Lorimer/Canadian Insti-
    tute for Economic Policy, Toronto, 1982).
Canada - House of Commons, Debates (1975).
Canadian Labour Congrss, 'Labour's Manifesto for
    Canada' (Canadian Labour Congress, Ottawa,
    1976).
Christofides, L.N. and D.A. Wilton, Wage Controls in
    Canada (1976:3 - 1978:2) A Study of Their
    Impact on Negotiated Base Wage Rates (Anti-
    Inflation Board, Ottawa, 1979).
Consultation and Consensus: A New Era in Policy
    Formulation (Conference Board in Canada,
    Ottawa, 1978).
Department of Consumer and Corporate Affairs Canada,
    Policies for Price Stability (Department of
    Consumer and Corporate Affairs, Ottawa, 1968).
Department of Finance Canada, 'Attack on Inflation:
    A Program of National Action,' (Department of
    Finance, Ottawa, 1975).
Department of Finance Canada, Economic Review
    (Department of Finance, Ottawa, April, 1978).
Haythorne, George V., 'Prices and Incomes Policy:
    The Canadian Experience, 1969-72,' Internation-
    al Labour Review, vol. 103 (1973) p. 485.
The Illusion of Wage and Price Control (The Fraser
    Institute, Vancouver, 1976).
'Industrial Relations after Wage and Price Controls
    Panel Discussion,' Canadian Public
    Policy/Analyse de Politiques, vol. 4 (1978), p.
    440.
McLeod, T.H., 'Anti-Inflation Administration: The
    Setting' (unpublished, 1979).
Maslove, Allan and Gene Swimmer, Wage Controls in
    Canada 1975-78: A Study of Public Decision-
    Making (Institute for Research on Public
    Policy, Montreal, 1980).
Ostry, Sylvia, Report of the Centre for the Study of
    Inflation and Productivity to the First Mini-
    sters' Conference (Economic Council of Canada,

142

Canada: The Perfect Environment?

Ottawa, November, 1978).

Prices and Incomes Commission, 'Inflation, Unemployment and Incomes Policy,' (Prices and Incomes Commission, Ottawa, 1972).

Smith, Douglas A., 'Wage Linkages between Canada and the United States,' Industrial and Labour Relations Review, vol. 29 (January, 1976), p. 258.

Staudohar, Paul, 'Effects of Wage and Price Controls in Canada, 1975-78,' Relations Industrielles/ Industrial Relations, vol. 34 (1979), p. 674.

Thompson, Mark, 'Restraint and Labour Relations: The Case of British Columbia,' Canadian Public Policy/Analyse de Politiques, vol. II (June, 1985), p. 171.

Thompson, Mark and Gene Swimmer (eds.), Conflict or Compromise: The Future of Public Sector Industrial Relations (Institute for Research on Public Policy, Montreal, 1984).

Wilson, T.A. and G.V. Jump, The Influence of the Anti-Inflation Program on Wages and Prices: A Simulation Analysis (Anti-Inflation Board, Ottawa, 1979).

Wood, W.D. and Pradeep Kumar (eds.), Canadian Perspective on Wage-Price Guidelines (Queen's University Industrial Relations Centre, Kingston, Ontario, 1976).

143

Chapter Five

THE FEDERAL REPUBLIC OF GERMANY: LIFE WITHOUT AN
INCOMES POLICY

Hans J. Michelmann

INTRODUCTION

To assert that the economic performance of the
Federal Republic of Germany (FRG) in the decades
since its establishment in 1949 has been the envy of
the world is almost a truism. The FRG, in addition
to its record of economic growth and strong export
performance, has had, with Switzerland, the lowest
inflation rate of any member of the OECD.[1] Such
achievements came without a great deal of government
intervention and, particularly important in the
present context, without a statutory income policy.
    This   chapter will explore the reasons for
Germany's remarkable performance in controlling
inflation in the absence of direct government
intervention in the income policy sector. The basic
argument will be that the FRG's success in this
regard has been in good part due to its harmonious
system of industrial relations, and especially to
the restraint exercised by the unions in that
context. Hence the chapter will begin by examining
the historical, societal and legal-institutional
settings of German industrial relations and the
characteristics of the unions that make them
moderate in the collective bargaining context. The
discussion of government incomes policy, a term of
questionable usefulness for much of FRG history,
will be divided into three sub-sections, corresponding to three periods since 1949 that have been
characterised by varying economic conditions and
different approaches by government toward influenc-
ing income developments as a means to stabilising
the economy. The final section will attempt to draw
some general conclusions about the German experience
with incomes policy.

144

Germany: Life Without an Incomes Policy

THE HISTORICAL AND INSTITUTIONAL SETTINGS

In the late 1940s, following the total collapse of
the Third Reich and in the context of the general
rebuilding of German society associated with the
forging of the Federal Republic, German leaders had
an opportunity to readjust, if not fundamentally
recast, many of their social, economic and political
institutions.   This   reconstruction   was   clearly
influenced by the negative experience with the Nazi
order and by many of the perceived shortcomings of
the preceding Weimar Republic.   These negative
examples predisposed the German leadership to shy
away from the command economy which was a feature of
the Hitler era, but also to view negatively the
ideological discord and social as well as political
fragmentation of Weimar. The recast institutions of
the postwar period reflected the attempt to combine
order, harmony and the desire for consensus - all
traditional features of German political culture and
features that remain strongly in evidence today -
with the liberal democratic ethos of the new republic.   The realisation that the widespread negative
attitudes toward the Weimar Republic had contributed
to that regime's collapse led to a strong resolve by
German elites, including those of labour and industry, to support the new state and its institutions.
A further carryover from the past, the propensity by
Germans to resort to legalistic solutions to the
settling of social and political conflict, is also a
prominent characteristic of FRG institutions, and
has had a strong impact on West German industrial
relations.
    A contemporary negative example, the German
Democratic Republic, helped discredit Communist and
other radically left-wing economic and political
schemes and thus to channel German collective life
along centrist or moderately conservative paths.
This   moderate   to   conservative   orientation   was
reflected in and reinforced by a period of centre-
right rule in the 1949-1966 period, which saw
coalition governments dominated by the right-of-
centre CDU-CSU Christian Democratic party coalition,
supported for much of the period by the centrist
(liberal) FDP. The reigning consensus in German
political culture induced the left-of-centre SPD
(Social Democratic) party to adopt the Bad Godesberg
Programme which purged the party of its Marxist
orientation and rhetoric.   The programme committed
the SPD   to a mixed, competitive economy and
de-emphasised collective economic policies.   Hence,

when the SPD joined the CDU-CSU in a Grand Coalition
in 1966, and then itself became the senior partner
in a left-of-centre coalition with the FDP in 1969,
the transition marked a shift in economic emphasis
but not a major departure from previous economic
policy.   Indeed, the whole period from 1949 to the
present has seen a remarkable consensus among the
major German groups on the basic premises of
economic policy, a consensus that was stronger than
in most, if not all, other West European countries.[2]

The exceptional conditions of the FRG's first
years had an, especially strong impact on the
structuring of economic institutions and organisations and on how they functioned during their crucial formative years.[3]   The need to rebuild Germany
after the widespread destruction of the Second World
War led to an all-encompassing emphasis on production and investment and a de-emphasis of distribution and the divisiveness that struggles over shares
of the economic pie can engender.   Hence a climate
of co-operation between the two sides of industry
developed in which industrial action was not considered an acceptable practice.   This climate of
co-operation helped contribute to the FRG consensus
on further development of the German welfare state
with its benefits for labour, and on the mix of economic and social policies which became known as the
'social market economy', associated with the long-
time Economics Minister Ludwig Erhard.   That
policy's success in fostering a long period of substantial economic growth with its attendant real
growth in income gave workers a stake in the German
economy and reinforced the feeling that such rewards
were possible only in a prospering economy that was
not seriously disrupted by labour strife resulting
from excessive union demands.   Avoidance of industrial conflict was also a result of the realisation
by employers and unions alike that the German
economy was heavily dependent on exports for its
prosperity and that export markets could be very
easily lost through unreliable delivery caused by
labour unrest.

Another factor making for union moderation was
their close, though unofficial, relationship with
the SPD.   While the German Trade Union Federation,
the Deutscher Gewerkschaftsbund (DGB), is officially
politically neutral and while there are no formal
organisational links with the SPD, the two organisations work closely together and a large percentage
of SPD deputies, in 1969 fully 91 percent, are union
members.[4]   This relationship proved crucial for

union moderation during periods of economic difficulty.   In 1966, following the FRG's first recession, the formation of the Grand Coalition strengthened labour's trust in government handling of the
economy.   By the time of the more severe economic
shocks resulting from the OPEC induced oil price increases, the SPD was anchoring the centre-left
government which stayed in power until 1982.   The
unions, then, for a prolonged period had privileged
access to a governing party sympathetic to their
interests, and thus a strong inducement not to make
life unduly difficult for their political colleagues
in the economic policy area.   Even during periods of
centre-right government the unions had an ally in
the small but influential trade union wing of the
CDU.   In short, historical, economic and political
factors helped play their parts in bringing about
union moderation and peaceful industrial relations
in the FRG.

The nature of union organisation is also an
important factor leading to industrial peace.   We
have already seen that the DGB does not espouse a
political ideology and lacks official ties to a
political party.   These features were felt necessary
by the original union leaders who wished to create a
united workers' movement that could accommodate
under one umbrella all the factions that had
bedevilled the scene before 1933.   Keeping DGB unity
intact required maintaining a moderate stance toward
major issues; at the same time, potential apostates
valued a united workers' movement highly enough to
remain within the DGB framework.   There has been
only one exception to maintenance of DGB unity that
occurred in 1954 when many Catholic unionists left
the DGB in a dispute over political matters and
organised a German Christian Trade Union Movement,
which, however, has remained small and uninfluen-
tial.[5]   The only other unions of note in the FRG are
two white collar unions, the Deutsche Angestellten
Gewerkschaft (DAG), and the Deutscher Beamtenbund
(DBB) which organises primarily civil servants.   The
DGB, however, is by far the most prominent of these
organisations and takes the lead in private sector
industrial relations.   Its affiliates in the
government sector are as important in themselves as
the DBB, and salary negotiations in the public
sector affecting the senior level white collar civil
servants is, at any rate, subject to constraints
that make union action in this sector of only
marginal importance for the economy as a whole.

Organisational features lead to trade union

147

moderation in yet another way. The DGB is dependent on a consensus among its 17 component unions, hence its position is much more moderate than that of its most radical constituent organisation. This moderation is demonstrated by its eschewal of any radical class struggle doctrine or rhetoric and its acceptance of the social market economy. The unions' dual role as representatives of labour in social, economic and political discussions with government and as negotiators of collective agreements makes taking radical positions in either context more difficult than is the case for employers who are organised in three separate associations; as employers in the context of collective bargaining (Bund Deutscher Arbeitsgeber-Confederation of German Employers' Associations (BDA), as an industrial pressure group (Bund Deutscher Industrien-Confederation of German Industries (BDI)) and in the compulsory, public law Deutscher Industrie und Handelstag (DIHT), the German Chamber of Industry and Commerce. These separate organisations representing industry sometimes take positions of varying degrees of hostility towards the unions.[6]

Equally important is the nature of the membership at the DGB component union level. These unions organise all workers, regardless of trade or profession, in an industry. Hence there is no destabilising competition at the level of firms for workers' loyalty, and management faces only one organisation in the context of collective bargaining. Union attitudes are also moderated by their role as entrepreneurs; the DGB owns the FRG's fourth largest commercial bank, Europe's largest property developing firm, an insurance company and tourist, printing and advertising retail co-operatives.[7] Union leadership's management of these enterprises gives it considerable insight and feeling for what is acceptable and feasible in the market place and, therefore, in industrial relations.

Union participation in worker codetermination provides the opportunity for yet further insight into the economic pressures facing employers, and for a degree of say over what transpires in the firm, both factors making for moderation and responsible pay claims. Codetermination has been a feature of the German industrial scene for much of the post-war period and takes essentially two forms at the level of the individual firm. A federal law requires that each firm with five employees or more have a works council to which worker members are elected by the firm's employees. The council deals with a variety of issues including such matters as piecework remuneration, training, firings and issues of central importance such as major technical or commercial changes planned by the management. Normally more than eighty percent of worker representatives are union members.[8]

In firms of medium size, that is, with more than 500 employees, federal law mandates that one-third of the supervisory board, which oversees the management board that has responsibility for day-to-day running of the firm, be composed of employee representatives. For firms with more than 2000 employees there is numerical parity between representatives of employers and employees on the supervisory board, with the chairman (a representative of the employer) having a casting vote, and the firm's management employees being represented on the workers' side. Only for the firms in the coal and steel sector, now decreasingly important in the German economy, is there true parity between worker and employer representatives on the supervisory board. Hence codetermination has its limits as a mechanism for bringing to bear worker pressure on management. It cannot be conceived of as implying equal partnership of workers and management in the firm if only because of the legal limitation on the issues that can be raised in that context and because of the less than equal representation of workers on supervisory boards in all but the coal and steel firms.[9] But the mechanism has proven a viable conflict resolution device in German companies, it allows workers' concerns to be raised and represented in key structures of the firm to an extent that has few counterparts elsewhere, and it allows workers' representatives, most of whom are also union activists, to gain insights into the economic situation of the firm. It is generally conceded that this means of involving worker representatives in the affairs of companies has helped improve the German industrial relations climate by making it more co-operative than it might otherwise be.

The propensity in the FRG toward 'juridifying' social relations to a high degree, that is, toward resorting to legal regulation, and toward legal resolution of conflicts is quite pronounced in all aspects of the German industrial relations system. This begins with the guarantee of the standard liberal democratic freedom of association in the Basic Law's Article 9, which makes explicit reference to the freedom to 'form associations to safeguard and improve working conditions . . . to everyone and to all trades, occupations and professions.' Article 9, then, guarantees the right of employers to form associations and the right of workers to become union members, to work actively on behalf of unions but, by court interpretation, also to refuse to join unions and not to be penalised for such a decision by being excluded from a job or from benefits derived through union bargaining. The Basic Law enjoins the government to not undertake actions that ·interfere with worker or employer organisations except when their actions interfere with the rights of others, and protects these parties from actions by third parties meant to interfere with their existence. The relevant provisions of the Basic Law have been interpreted by the courts to mean that the government may not interfere with the process of collective bargaining. By thus guaranteeing the celebrated right to 'Tarifautonomie', the rights of economic organisations to arrive at pay rates through collective bargaining without interference, the courts have effectively ruled out the basis for a statutory incomes policy. The FRG's Constitutional Court has ruled, however, that this 'Tarifautonomie' is subject to the provisions of a legal framework for collective bargaining.

This legal framework is the Collective Agreements Act of 1949 as amended in 1969 and 1974.[10] It defines the parties that can engage in collective bargaining and makes attaining legal recognition as a bargaining association very difficult. More than ninety percent of all work contracts are made under the Act's provisions. Collective agreements are made up of two parts. A first part establishes obligations taken on by the two parties. The most important of these for industrial relations in the FRG is the peace obligation, which prohibits employees and employers from undertaking any action that has as its objective the changing of provisions of a valid collective agreement during the time it is in force, and the compliance obligation, which enjoins the bargaining parties to influence their members to abide by the agreement. The second, normative, part of collective agreements establishes their contents, including the provisions for implementation and termination of the covered contracts and sometimes provisions regarding the organisation of firms and works councils.[11] These norms are minimum conditions, covering the contracts of all firms subject to the agreement.

Under the provisions of the <u>Collective Agreements Act</u>, an agreement is a contract in writing under private law, ranking as a source of law after an Act of Parliament and a statutory regulation.[12] All contracts covered by a collective agreement are, hence, authoritatively altered by the agreement. Disputes regarding interpretation of the contract or alleged breaches are adjudicated by conciliation boards that are often established by the agreements and there is recourse to the extensive system of labour courts. Because the conditions of the agreement are treated as minimal norms which are negotiated by taking into account the situation of marginal firms in an industry, plant level agreements, negotiated subsequently between management and works council, may provide more generous terms and often lead to substantial wage drift. Arbitration procedures, usually based on a model agreement devised by the DGB and the BDA in 1954, are employed if negotiations are not productive. Only if no suggestions for settlement of a bargaining deadlock are arrived at through arbitration procedures or if the suggested settlement is not acceptable to both parties, is the peace obligation no longer in effect and measures of labour conflict may begin.

The extensive 'juridification' of German labour relations establishes the whole process in a well defined framework based on conservative assumptions that are meant to lead to harmony and balance between the two sides, and most importantly, to avoid conflict. Hence, strikes and lockouts are legal only as last resorts, after arbitration has failed. The criteria for a legal industrial action are very strict and the peace obligation is taken seriously. In a society where harmony, orderliness and consensus are so highly prized and resolution of conflict through legal channels is the accepted norm, it is impolitic to resort to quasi-legal methods in industrial relations, and any hint of illegality leads quickly to public disapproval. These features of FRG society and industrial relations also help to account for the comparatively high degree of German labour peace, and moderation in union pay demands.

Finally, a regularised pattern of bargaining, also conducive to moderate income claims by unions, developed early on, and has stayed in effect until the present. Industry-wide collective bargaining on a regional basis, with regions roughly corresponding to the German Laender (the German states), is the rule, although single firm agreements (for example, for the Volkswagenwerk) are not uncommon. The main activity of a firm determines which collective agreement it is subject to. There are two types of negotiations, talks on pay increases, usually held annually, and bargaining over working conditions such as hours of work and holiday pay which result in working agreements that cover several years. Representatives of the industrial union and the corresponding BDA representatives commence bargaining in one region, usually a fairly prosperous one, and the settlement reached is more or less closely followed by both sides in other regions. As a result, the confrontation between unions and employer representatives is usually limited to one bargaining region, and this helps reduce labour conflict. Frequently a key agreement, often that reached in the metalworking industry, sets the parameters for agreements reached in other industries.

Under normal circumstances, only organised workers and employers are affected by a collective agreement. The provisions of a collective agreement can, however, be applied to non-organised firms by the federal Minister of Labour and Social Affairs or by his delegates in the Laender after consultations with the unions and employer federation and with the representatives of the employers and workers to which the agreement is to be extended, providing that employers to whom the original agreement applies employ more than fifty percent of the industry's workers in the region and that without the extension to the unorganised sector, working conditions there would drop below acceptable levels. Approximately 20 percent of all workers, primarily in industries with numerous small firms, are covered by such extension agreements.[13]

GOVERNMENT AND INCOME DEVELOPMENTS

In the previous section it was noted that for legal and constitutional reasons there has not been a statutory income policy in the FRG. It should also be clear by now that resort to such a policy has not been necessary because of the features of the industrial relations system and the characteristics of union organisation and behaviour. Of course, this is not to imply that every government since 1949 has maintained a strictly laisse faire attitude toward income developments, particularly when inflation, to which there is such widespread public aversion, began to reach levels that, while acceptable elsewhere, were politically dangerous to a German government.

The history of government attempts to influence income developments can be divided into roughly three periods that are demarcated by changes in economic conditions, by changes in the economic philosophies of key government actors and the resulting changes in the propensity for government activism toward the economy, and by adjustments in government policy brought about as a result of government experience in attempting to affect income developments. At no time has a German government contemplated a resort to mandating pay rates by law; the action undertaken has always been indirect and has involved a combination of persuasion and resort to various fiscal measures. And, of course, there have been the interventions by the German Central Bank, the Deutsche Bundesbank (DBB), which have been as important as federal government action in affecting the main parameters of the FRG economy.

Period I, 1948-1966
The first years of the Federal Republic saw very little government intervention in the economy. The CDU-CSU dominated government continued the liberal economic approach adopted by the German authorities in 1948, even before the FRG's founding, and the economy, freed from the constraints of the pre-1948 period, responded dramatically. A widespread con-sensus on the need for reconstruction extended to the economic policy sphere, especially since the policies adopted by Ludwig Erhard, who managed the economy first as Economics Minister from 1949 until 1963, and then as Chancellor until 1966, fostered strong growth. During the 1950s there was neither a concerted counter-cyclical policy nor any developed conception of a government incomes policy.[14]

Incomes policy as a means to control inflation was, at any rate, unnecessary during the 1950s be-cause of a unique combination of factors. Although the economy was growing rapidly, unemployment was high. Inflation did not exist, for all practical purposes, after 1951, and prices actually dropped in 1953. Between 1954 and 1960, the mean annual rate of price increases was 1.6 percent.[15] Because of the emphasis by the government on fostering exports and on low consumption and because of the compara-tive weakness of unions due to unemployment caused largely by the continuing influx of refugees from the German Democratic Republic, employers were

reluctant to allow any wage increases at all, and
unions had to struggle to establish the principle of
an annual wage increase.[16]

By the mid-1950s, conditions had changed somewhat. The unions had improved their bargaining
strategy vis-a-vis the BDA; rather than allowing the
regional union organisations to bargain on their
own, concerted strategies were now being developed
at the centre and imposed on the regions. Further,
the economy was particularly buoyant and real wage
rates increased on average by 4.8 percent from 1955
to 1958, slightly more rapidly than growth in
productivity. Such increases were not inflationary
because savings rose appreciably at the same time.
Employers conceded the large wage increases because,
beginning in 1956, there were the first signs of the
labour shortages that characterised the FRG in the
1960s.

Conditions of economic boom continued and the
mark was revalued in 1961, leading to a lowered
growth rate and a tougher employer attitude toward
wage increases. Notwithstanding this, real wages
rose at an average rate of 6.5 percent between 1959
and 1962, again outstripping gains in productivity,
and bringing about cost-push inflation in 1961 and
1962 of 2.3 and 3 percent.[17] These conditions
prompted calls for state controls over unions which
were not heeded by Erhard, though he did openly
raise the possibility of adopting Taft-Hartley-like
measures in an attempt to pressure unions to put off
threatened strikes.

The late fifties and early sixties also saw
attempts at formulating principles to guide pay
increases. The Bundesbank's President, Karl
Blessing, asked to devise guidelines for pay
increases compatible with price stability, proposed
in 1960 that price stability could be maintained if
wages did not rise more than productivity. But in
attempting to suggest how such an approach might be
applied in the upcoming wage rounds, he destroyed
its credibility by grossly underpredicting actual
productivity gains. As a result, Erhard returned to
the previous approach of asking unions to moderate
their pay demands in the interest of the general
welfare, but his intervention through persuasion was
not effective, as we have seen by the figures for
1961 and 1962.

In the absence of effective government intervention, the steel industry's employer organisation
in 1962 resolved to toughen its stand in the trend-
setting bargaining round with the metal workers'

union. Faced with a demand for a ten percent pay increase, a decrease in working time and increased holidays, the employers offered three percent, but then compromised by granting six percent and longer vacations when the unions threatened industrial action.[18]

The pattern of confrontation between the two sides repeated itself in 1963 under conditions of an economic downturn but continuing inflation. Erhard, backed by the news media, urged union moderation, and in accordance with the productivity-based pay increase formula, suggested increases of 3.5 percent, the estimated productivity increase for the next year. Several rounds of negotiations in the metalworking industry, again involved in the pattern-setting bargaining round, left the two sides in that industry far apart and the unions opted for selective strikes in the affected region's largest and most strongly unionised firms. The employers retaliated with a region-wide lockout, whereupon the unions decided to strike in the FRG's Northrhine-Westfalia industrial heartland. Government intervention took the form of inviting both sides to Bonn, where a compromise pay settlement, still exceeding the productivity-based formula's guidelines, was reached.[19]

The ensuing wage rounds, again settled essentially in the pace-setting metal industry talks, were significantly affected by negative reaction to union militancy by the public, the press and even by the SPD, now in its post-Bad Godesberg period of moderation. The subsequent two pay rounds saw the metalworkers agree to a delay in the implementation of a reduced work week in return for a 7.5 percent pay increase and additional holiday time. In 1965, a new pay increase formula, suggested by an independent arbiter, H. Meinhold, and calling for pay increases amounting to the sum of productivity gains plus the projected inflation rate formed the basis of a settlement. The Meinhold formula, as it came to be known, gained tacit acceptance by unions and employers as an equitable approach to settling future pay disputes.

The government's basically non-interventionist approach to income determination in the years until 1966 were consistent with the CDU-CSU's emphasis on letting the price mechanism regulate the economy. This liberal approach did not, of course, prescribe total government inattention to developments in the economy, because minimal conditions had to be established to allow the price mechanism to work effectively.[20] Hence an <u>Act Prohibiting Constraints on Competition</u> was passed in 1957.

More important for developments regarding income and inflation was the establishment in the same year of the German Central Bank, the Deutsche Bundesbank (DBB). It was created by merging the banks of the Laender and the pre-existing federal level Bank deutscher Laender. The federal government proposes eight members of the DBB's Central Council and each of the eleven Laender has the right to propose one. This method of appointment has contributed to the DBB maintaining a high degree of independence from the federal government in its primary task of maintaining a stable Deutschmark. Its secondary task is to assist the federal government's economic policy, but should the two goals be in conflict, monetary stabilisation is to prevail.[21] The degree of consensus among private sector groups, the political parties and government officals on the principle of Bundesbank independence and on its priorities has been remarkable even in periods when the bank's policies contradicted the interests and conceptions of some or all of these parties. But this consensus helps to explain the bank's success in its stabilisation efforts which, indirectly of course, have had a considerable impact on income developments in the FRG.

Another government measure in 1957, this time of more direct effect for the income policy sector, was a law for the indexation with a time lag of the level of retirement pensions to the development of earnings in the working population.[22] This was part of the building of the German welfare state that has helped to develop a strong social consensus by providing benefits for the working population, but because of its cost implications, it also entailed the possibility of inflationary consequences.

Germany's participation in the various schemes of European integration, the European Coal and Steel Community in 1952 and the European Economic Community in 1958, was to have a substantial impact especially since the free movement of goods and services as well as capital and labour associated with these communities opened up her economy to outside economic pressures that were not possible to control through strictly national measures. But participation in the European institutions also had an impact on the development of German economic views. Economics Minister Erhard vigorously resisted the Keynesian approach to economic policy that was prevalent in Brussels, but he could not

prevent the development of medium-term action
programmes in that context which, in turn, helped
induce greater discussion of cyclical and fiscal
policy in the FRG.

As part of its reaction to these discussions,
the federal government in 1963 established a Council
of Economic Experts, composed of academic
economists, which was to report annually to
Parliament on the performance of the German economy.
The Council soon developed a reputation of
independence from the government and, though not
allowed to recommend specific policy measures, has
had considerable impact on the economic scene
because of the quality of its work and because the
federal government must reply to the report in the
Bundestag, the FRG's lower house of Parliament. One
of the report's sections deals with income
developments and the share of national income going
to wage and salary earners.

The Council has set out guidelines for
acceptable pay increases which have had considerable
moral authority. In the same vein, it gave its
approval to the Meinhold formula and based its
suggestions for the level of pay increases in 1966
on that method of calculation. This formula formed
the basis of the Council's pay recommendations for
the ensuing years. In its 1965 report, the Council
proposed the creation of an institution which it
called 'concerted action' to help develop an incomes
policy that was conducive to price stability. It
was to be a forum in which the representatives of
the state and the private sector could meet to
exchange information and plan to co-ordinate their
action to achieve that goal.

In its subsequent reports, the Council reiter-
ated the call for continued exchanges of information
about the parties' medium-term objectives that would
allow them to adjust their behaviour. The mutual
justification of their proposed actions would allow
all to see the economic situation more clearly and
to realise that unjustified claims by any of them
could lead to attempts by the others to regain or
improve their own positions. Such a distribution
struggle would lead to inflation detrimental to
everyone. Hence exchanges of information and the
adjustment of participants' action to take into
account the interests and points of view of other
actors would lead to the desired consensus and to
stability. This message, repeated by the Council a
number of times, was to become the philosophy of
legally institutionalised concerted action shortly

157

to be established.

The Erhard government's reaction in early 1966 to the Council's suggestion about concerted action was negative. However, inflation was increasing to 3.3 percent in 1966 as a result of the Erhard government's stimulation of the economy in preparation for an impending election, and by September, 1966, Erhard had submitted to Parliament a bill to further economic stability. It was too little too late and as the Bundesbank's restrictive monetary policy, intended to curb the inflationary pressures, reined in the economy, the Federal Republic slid into its first-ever recession, at the same time as the federal budget went into strong deficit. The crisis led to the Erhard government's resignation and the establishment of the Grand Coalition.

Dr. Karl Schiller, Germany's leading Keynesian, became Economic Minister. The appointment ushered in a new era of German economic policy. Because there was widespread agreement that monetary policy, as administered by the Bundesbank, had been insufficient to maintain an adequately functioning economy, there was now support for a more inter-ventionist stance and an end to the era of liberal economics.

Period II: 1967 to 1973
Before 1967 it is not possible to speak of an incomes policy in the FRG. As we have seen, the government chose to stay at the margin of the pay negotiation process, intervening only to exhort moderation, or to mediate between the two sides 'at signs of stalemate. But with the coming to power of the Grand Coalition, the approach changed. There was still no attempt to intervene directly in the sense of legislating particular pay settlements. But the tone was set when in February, 1967, heeding the advice of the Council of Economic Experts, Schiller called into session the first meeting of concerted action consisting of representatives of government, industry and labour. This was to be the first of a series of meetings that continued for over ten years, and had as one of its main objects the moderation of pay increases as a measure of economic stabilisation.

Concerted action was given its legal basis with the passage in June, 1967 of the Stability and Growth Act, a package of measures designed to provide the government levers to fine-tune the

economy.[23] The Act's global goals were the same as
those stipulated as the rationale for establishing
the Council of Economic Experts, viz., the
maintenance of price stability, a high level of
employment, a positive balance of payments and
adequate growth. Specifically, the Act, which is
still in effect, obligates the government to provide
a yearly economic report. The Act then sets out the
legal basis for a Keynesian economic policy by
providing for countercyclical budget and fiscal
policy, for the laying aside of government funds
during times of economic boom to be spent in
recessions, for medium-term finance and investment
planning to take into account cyclical variations in
demand, for varying taxation of income and wealth,
and for fostering private sector investment. Its
provisions regarding concerted action are set out in
Section 3 of the Act, which provides that should one
of the Act's four goals be endangered, the federal
government is to establish economic 'orientation
data' for a simultaneous adjustment of action
(concerted action) by local governments, unions and
employer organisations to achieve the Act's goals.
The orientation data are, in particular, to provide
a representation of the overall economic
interconnections relevant to any situation. The
Economics Minister is to explain these data at the
request of any of the participants.

The history of concerted action over the next
years is the history of government income policy
during the same period.[24] Its author, Economics
Minister Karl Schiller, wished to use it as a
mechanism of demand management in the context of his
overall Keynesian approach to German economic
policy. Given 'Tarifautonomie', direct measures to
limit income developments were lacking. With
concerted action, just as the Council of Economic
Experts had suggested, the two sides of industry
could be enlightened on the consequences of their
planned action, and could be influenced, while
retaining strict 'autonomy', to orient their
interests and actions towards the general good.
Schiller, in other words, wished to institutionalise
and intensify the process of moral suasion to which
the previous governments had limited their
intervention in the pay bargaining rounds and to
develop the process into a permanent dialogue
between government and the two sides of industry in
which he could attempt to persuade them to support
his policies. In that sense, Schiller's concerted
action was a step beyond the recommendations of the

159

Council of Economic Experts, who had seen it only as a crisis management mechanism.

To persuade them to co-operate, Schiller promised the unions that concerted action would allow them to participate in the development of economic and social policy. The employers were led to believe that concerted action would result in guidelines for pay increases arrived at through a co-operative process, and hence to a limitation of union claims. In response to many requests that the goals of concerted action be formally specified, Schiller replied that these matters were spelled out sufficiently clearly in the Act. By the time that the participants had grasped the nature of the process, that is, a means by the government to solicit support of its economic goals, concerted action had become sufficiently established and accepted by the public that withdrawal by any of its participants would have been politically harmful to that participant.

The unions were, at any rate, inclined to accept concerted action as part of the Keynesian approach to economic policy that they had officially espoused in the DGB's 1963 program. Being asked to participate in the making of economic policy at the highest level was, for them, a significant improvement of status. Further, they hoped to affect the distribution of national income in their favour and to have the redistribution sanctioned by a public sector institution. More immediately relevant practical results could be forthcoming also since the unions would have access to information in the context of concerted action which had not been available to them before, and they would be able to assess employer intentions so that they could maximise worker interests in the pay bargaining rounds.

The employer organisations were initially not favourably disposed toward Schiller's economic policies because they feared the interventionist implications of these policies. However, they welcomed the idea of an incomes policy, which was what Schiller emphasised as the essence of concerted action in his approach to them, since it would make wage developments more predictable. Further, they hoped, through concerted action, to institutionalise the concept of productivity-based incomes policy supported by the Council of Economic Experts. Whereas the unions hoped to change the distribution of income in their favour, the employer organisations hoped to institutionalise existing

shares. Hence the employers continued to insist on
limiting concerted action discussions to strictly
economic matters, a position that was in line with
their interests in persuading the unions to limit
their pay claims. Right at the outset, then, there
were conflicting views concerning the nature of
concerted action, with each of the three main
participants, government, employers and unions,
having quite different conceptions. This was not
the most auspicious basis for an institution that
was meant to lead to an adjustment of action through
accommodation of individual interests to the general
good.

Schiller invited mainly the participants in
collective bargaining to the first concerted action
meetings. The three major business groupings, BDA,
BDI and DIHT, as well as representatives of the
wholesale and exporter and the trade and artisanate
associations, made up the employers' side. On the
union side, the DGB, slightly less than half its
component unions and the DAG were represented. The
public sector contingent consisted of the Minister,
his advisers and the president of the cartel office.
Finally, there were representatives of the Council
of Economic Experts. Over the ensuing years, the
Minister also invited representatives of the retail
trade association, the president of the Bundesbank,
as well as representatives of the farmers' union,
credit institutions, the DBB, consumer representatives and a number of others.

Concerted action meetings were chaired by the
Minister of Economics, and took place from three to
six times annually. Before long, there was
contention over the agenda which led to the practice
of having it established by committee rather than by
the Minister. The unions, in line with their
expectations regarding concerted action, wished to
broaden the discussions beyond incomes policy to
include fundamental social issues, whereas the
employers insisted on concentrating exclusively on
economic issues narrowly defined. In the event, the
discussions were broadened beyond strictly incomes
and conjunctural policy themes.

One of the key ambiguities of the whole
exercise was the status of the orientation data to
be provided by the government. The Act stated that
these target figures for economic performance were
to be provided by the Minister but the question of
the extent of their binding nature was soon raised.
The choice of the concept 'orientation data' had
been based on the need to assure both sides of

161

industry that 'Tarifautonomie' would be respected;
the term 'guidelines', preferred initially by the
SPD was dropped because it implied regulation, which
was incompatible with 'Tarifautonomie' and unacceptable to workers and employers. From the first
meeting it was clear that the orientation data would
not be viewed as binding by the private sector but
considered mainly as broad goals to be taken into
account in collective bargaining. Interpretation in
the press and explicit statements by government
officials which implied expectations that the two
sides should seek to approximate the income goals in
the pay rounds were emphatically rejected by the
unions.

Further, although Schiller had attempted to
leave the impression that the orientation data were
to be established in the course of the concerted
action sessions, the government in fact devised and
presented them. Hence, before long, the other
participants came to realise that, despite their
expectations, they were not to have direct influence
on government policy through concerted action. The
unions were soon to learn that the orientation data
represented goals which the government wanted to
have the economy attain whereas they had wished to
see orientation data developed in the context of
concerted action as determinative parameters for
government economic policy.

These government orientation data proved
frequently to be unrealistic indicators of economic
trends. The public, however, was generally unaware
of the true nature of these figures, interpreting
them as authoritative predictors of future economic
developments and expecting them to be heeded in
collective bargaining. Pressure created by the
public's expectations made it very difficult for
unions and employers alike to deviate from the
government figures, and the government made it no
easier for them by predicting negative economic
consequences should the figures not be heeded, hence
implicitly assessing blame to the non-compliant in
advance.

Schiller's practice of publicising precise
figures for pay increases when elaborating on
concerted action meetings to the press, more precise
than the global figures that the participants had
accepted in the meetings, created a great deal of
controversy. Schiller hoped to influence collective
bargaining in this way, but both employers and
unions protested at what they saw as unacceptable
interference. Despite such protests, the government

162

persisted in publishing very precise figures for the pay developments it wished to see realised, and stopped this practice only after the unions threatened to cease participating in concerted action.

Both unions and employers repeatedly requested that they participate in establishing the orientation data in the first years of concerted action, but they were allowed by the government only to accept or reject the government's figures in the joint communiques issued after each session and not even to comment on these figures. Hence, beginning in 1969 the unions, and a year later the employers, issued their own estimates of future economic trends, thereby undermining the authority of the government's projections.

From 1970 onwards, income orientation data became less precise, the government limiting itself to issuing a global figure for the overall increase in income for wage and salary earners from which, because of wage drift, it was impossible to derive exact pay increase figures. Notwithstanding this, both government and employers continued to make reference to these data as upper limits to pay increases. On the workers' side, however, particularly among the rank and file, the tendency developed to see the government's income figures as minimum values and to evaluate the performance of union leaders by the extent to which collective bargaining led to increases above these values. This effect was, of course, the precise opposite of what had been intended as an exercise to stabilise the economy through moderating pay claims.

Concerted action received its first practical test in the attempts to pull the German economy out of the 1966-67 economic downturn. The government initiated stimulative measures and the DGB, not wishing to damage the recovery and wishing to show good faith, recommended that the orientation figures be heeded. In the event, pay raises averaged 3.5 percent, unions put off renegotiating a large number of expired contracts, and the economic decline was arrested.[25]

Assessment of economic prospects continued to be negative, however, and this was reflected in the orientation data for 1968. The unions again exercised restraint in their pay demands, and this brought promises by Schiller that they would be rewarded for their sacrifices when the economy improved.[26] Unfortunately, the government figures were already out of date when the collective

agreements were signed - the economy was already
undergoing a.strong recovery. As a result, profits
had risen dramatically at the end of 1968 while
wages and salaries reflected union restraint.[27] The
year 1969 saw similar developments; there was unprecedented economic growth but pay lagged far behind
as a result of the low 1968 pay settlements.[28] This
resulted in general discontent among the worker rank
and file that boiled over into wildcat strikes in
fall 1969. Union leaders quite naturally saw these
as a threat to their own positions and hence fought
hard for pay increases in the ensuing pay rounds.

There followed five very high pay raises of
14.7, 11.8, 9.0, 12.0 and 11.4 percent for the years
1970 through 1974 despite repeated government calls
for restraint.[29] Rank and file militancy and a
tight labour market made it impossible for union
leaders to exercise restraint even had they wanted
to. The unions had lost faith in concerted action,
and the spirit of co-operation among its
participants was gone. There was increasing
complaint among them about the irrelevance of the
exercise but because of public support for and
belief in the institution, engendered in part by the
recovery in 1968 and 1969, in part by the publicity
surrounding the meetings, neither unions nor
employers withdrew for fear of the resulting
negative public reaction.

Thus, although it was clear that their
practical purpose of moderating pay demands had been
severely undermined, meetings continued. For the
government, concerted action provided a platform
where its policies could be publicly presented and
where it could be seen to be consulting with the
important private actors. By participating in
concerted action, it was more difficult for
employers and unions to attack government
polemically; this may well have contributed to a
calmer and more objective economic debate. It was
also easier for government to escape blame for
economic problems if the private sector participants
did not follow the orientation data it provided.

When Schiller resigned in 1972, concerted
action lost more of its significance because of his
close association with it. After the November, 1972
elections, the economics portfolio was assigned to
Hans Friderichs, an FDP minister, whose party's
economic policy and negative attitudes toward unions
further alienated labour. In the subsequent economic crisis years of 1974 and 1975, the government
began to turn its back on Keynesianism and returned

164

to a reliance on market forces to regulate the
economy. The meetings of concerted action, now of
much less significance to the government than before, continued for a number of years. Efforts were
made to revive concerted action in the late seventies, but the unions were increasingly critical,
particularly of the Council of Economic Experts'
participation and the neoclassical stance it adopted
in its reports. The unions officially withdrew from
concerted action in 1977, citing as their reason
their dissatisfaction with the process and their
anger at the employer organisations, who had
challenged the Schmidt government's 1976 codetermination legislation in the Constitutional Court.

The government subsequently fulfilled its
obligation to inform the major economic groupings of
developments in the economy through bilateral
meeting with the DGB, the other unions and the
employer groups in which the Chancellor frequently
participates. The discussions with the unions have
become more difficult with the return of a CDU-CSU
dominated government in fall 1982. But even
meetings with other groups are not particularly
successful; they usually bring an exchange of
information and views, but no concrete results. The
prospects for a more highly coordinated approach to
solving economic problems among governments, the
employers and the unions, a development desired by
the economics ministry, are not good. The unions
have been unwilling to return to concerted action,
and employer groups are also not enthusiastic.
Hence the government has returned to attempts to
influence the private sector through less
institutionalised moral suasion, as practised in the
years before 1967, and to the blunt instrument of
restrictive monetary policy.

Period III: 1974 to the Present
As we have seen, the years from 1969 to 1974 were
years of high pay increases. The aggressive pay
bargaining by the unions during this period
increased labour's share of GDP from an average of
70.5 percent in the 1960's to 72 percent in 1972-73
and 74 percent in 1974-75.[30] A good deal of the
unions' motivation for their behaviour in this
context can be attributed to the need to make up for
the relative losses of the recession and post-
recession periods, but later it was clear that an
inflationary psychology had set in engendered in
part by the unusually high price increases during

these years.   Inflation grew from 1.9 percent in
1969 to 3.3 percent in 1970, 5.2 percent in 1971 and
5.6 percent in 1972.   In 1973 it reached 7.0 percent, the highest level until then in the FRG.
     The public authorities recognised that some-
thing had to be done.   Despite Bundesbank and federal government warnings that high pay settlements
would not be sustainable and would put jobs at risk,
the DGB's public sector union, engaged in 1974 in
the pace-setting pay round, bargained intransigent-
ly, and, after a number of selective strikes, won
pay increases in the 12-15 percent range.   Settlements in other sectors, although not all of the same
magnitude, followed the trend.   Clearly the wage-
price spiral was in danger of getting out of control.   The choices for Bundesbank and federal
government were to allow the wage increases to work
their way through the economy into ever accelerating
prices, or to put a stop to the process by applying
an even more stringent monetary policy.   They opted
for the latter course, and inflation, rather than
shooting into the double digit range, remained, as
in the previous year, at 7.0 percent.
     The results of the 1974 actions were
predictable.   Because of the restrictive monetary
policies, firms were unable to pass on in higher
prices the costs engendered by the pay increases,
and numerous employers found that they could deal
with these costs only by cutting back on their
labour force.[31]   Hence unemployment increased to 2.6
percent (about one million), a level unheard of in
the FRG for fifteen years.   Unemployment was to
persist from 1974 on, hovering in the four percent
range until 1980, when it began another upsurge that
levelled out in 1983 and 1984 at 9.1 percent.[32]
     The 1975 Budget Structure Act gave further
evidence of the shift in government emphasis.   It
called for a reduction in the public debt and cut
back the more generous provisions of the government's unemployment programmes introduced in the
1969 Work Promotion Act.   This Act had initiated
generous worker re-education schemes and job
training programmes as well as other measures to
deal with structural unemployment.   Henceforth it
would be more difficult to turn down jobs offered by
the employment offices and still to qualify for
unemployment insurance.[33]   Subsequent government
actions reined these programmes in even further.
     Not surprisingly, such measures, the implicit
shift in government emphasis away from full
employment evidenced by the 1974 policies and the

166

continuing reliance by the government and Bundesbank
on monetary policy to control the economy, created a
great stir. The unions complained of having become
the victims of the policy to control inflation. The
restraint they exercised in subsequent pay rounds
(wages and salaries increased on average by 6.3
percent from 1975 to 1979[34] while labour's share of
GDP dropped to 70 percent in 1978)[35] is in large
part due to the factors spelled out earlier in this
chapter. But it can also be attributed to the fact
that the SPD-FDP Schmidt government, made up largely
of ministers holding trade union membership, was
able to persuade the unions that any larger
increases would lead only to higher unemployment.
The restrictive monetary policies of the public
authorities, henceforth signalled annually by the
Bundesbank's practice of publishing figures for the
coming year's growth in the money supply to guide
salary and price increases, and the government's
campaign of persuasion, worked reasonably effectively to stamp out the inflation psychology of the
early to mid-1970's.

The corollary of restrictive monetary policy
was rather modest economic growth which the government attempted to accelerate somewhat in order to
improve labour market conditions. In 1977, the
government initiated a program of public investment
in infrastructure, energy saving and environmental
projects, providing a stimulus which led to a
noticeable increase in the growth rate,[36] but this
was to be the last government-provided stimulus of
the decade. Some tax cuts and an easing of monetary
policy in the late 1970's, also to improve the
labour market and to reward the unions for their pay
bargaining restraint as well as to give in to international pressure that Germany help lead an economic
recovery, had to be reversed after the second oil
shock, and restrictive fiscal and monetary policies
returned.

These policies have been reasonably successful
in helping keep inflation under control. The
restrictive policies implemented in 1974 were
followed by a decline from the 1974 inflation rate
of 7.0 percent to a 6.1 percent rate in 1975, a 4.4
percent rate in 1976 and an average rate of 3.3
percent in the following three years while wages and
salaries increased by an average of 6.4 percent for
the same period.[37] It will be remembered that these
years saw the growth of unemployment to the four
percent range.

By the late seventies, the unions had fully

accepted that unemployment was a problem of central
concern and that it was not solely a cyclical
problem but had other, structural and technological,
roots.   Their   policy   recommendations   to   the
government and their shift in bargaining emphasis
reflected this change in analysis.   This is not to
imply an abandonment of their long-held view that
insufficient demand   is   a   major   cause   for   the
conditions that had led to higher unemployment.
They   have   consistently   asked   for   government
stimulation of the economy, requests that were met
in   the   mid-   to   late   seventies   by   the   special
investment program and tax cuts.   They have also
persisted in their demand for more global steering
of the economy in an 'economic framework plan' which
would   involve   the   local   and   national   political
authorities as well as the unions in the co-ordination   of   economic   development   projects   at   the
regional and sectoral levels, especially with the
aim of fostering greater employment.[38]   Their suggestions for dealing with structural unemployment
also called for more targetted government help to
particularly severely affected regions and sectors
and public investment in the health sector, on
environmental projects, in social services and in
housing.[39]   To make investment more socially responsible, particularly to have investment projects
reflect   the   need   for   increased   employment,   the
unions   have   called   for   'Investitionslenkung,'
guidance   of   investment,   involving   investment
registry   centres   staffed   by   representatives   of
government, industry and unions, to which all major
investment   projects   would   be   reported.   Final
decision would, however, be left to the private
sector.[40]
    Humanisation of work became a major theme in
response to the problems of technological change.
Hence   unions   demanded   increased   provision 'for
retraining, improved working conditions, security of
employment provisions, improved safety provisions
and, of central importance to income policy, a
shortening of maximum working time.[41]   As we shall
see, this goal, in particular, was pursued with
great vigour in subsequent collective bargaining
rounds.
    Finally, the unions continued to espouse their
wage-consumption theory.   They have argued that
demand could be injected into the economy through a
high wage policy that would bring more consumption,
hence more demand, more growth and lower unemployment.[42]   This analysis has not met with a positive

response by the employers, because like other union
demands, it was made in an economic context not
favourable to large scale cost increases for
employers.

The second OPEC-induced oil price increase
contributed to a substantial reduction in the German
growth rate. In 1979 it had still been at a
respectable four percent, but the following year it
dropped to 1.9 percent, only to go into the negative
range at -0.2 and -1.1 for 1981 and 1982,
respectively. When growth returned, it was at the
puny rate of 1.3 percent for 1983 and 2.6 percent
for 1984. Clearly, even if economic policy kept the
inflation rate to respectable figures when compared
to other countries (1979 - 3.9 percent, 1980 - 5.3
percent, 1981 - 6.3 percent, 1982 - 5.4 percent,
1983 - 3.2 percent and 1984 - 2.4 percent), this was
not a time for major pay claims, especially since
unemployment was increasing from 3.8 percent in 1980
to 5.5 percent in 1981, 7.5 percent in 1982 and 9.1
percent in both 1983 and 1984.[43]

Collective bargaining rounds were, as a result,
burdened with discussions over shares of a slower
growing or, in some years, shrinking pie. The 1980
round was held in the context of reasonable profits
in 1979, although the effects of imported inflation
through higher oil prices were beginning to show.
In the event, average wages and prices increased by
seven percent, a rate that was higher than those of
the previous two years.[44] In the following year, a
five percent increase in wages and salaries resulted
after long disputes between employers, who wished to
see increases limited to productivity gains, and the
unions, who argued strenuously for increases commen-
surate with the rise in prices. As it was, inflation outpaced income gains and workers experienced a
real decline in income. But employers were no
better off, as profits fell, in large part due to
developments in the export market.[45]

The picture improved for employers in 1982,
when profits improved, but for workers, the average
increase of four percent left them less well off in
real terms than in the previous year, though productivity improved. Notwithstanding these developments, the Council of Economic Experts called for a
continuing lag of wage increases behind productivity
gains to help diminish the high unemployment rate.
At the same time the Council argued that profits had
not recovered sufficiently in 1982, nor had they
made up for the low rates in previous years to
encourage investment requisite for increasing

employment. Employers and unions would have to determine 'on the market' which wage and salary rate increase would be consistent with increased employment.[46]

The pay round of 1983 led to an even lower settlement at 3.2 percent than in the previous year. Further, workers were confronted with increased unemployment insurance payments, pension contributions and taxes, leaving their take-home pay unchanged from 1982 and their real income noticeably lower. With productivity again higher, profits rose substantially.[47]

The trend of these developments, particularly the rise in unemployment and the decline in worker income, did not go unchallenged by the unions. They were incensed that the cutbacks workers had had to take were not leading to the investment that was the rationale cited by the DBA, some leading public officials and the Council of Economic Experts for the need for wage restraint.[48] Continuing arguments about overpriced labour, they claimed, could not be substantiated by economic data, which indicated that real wage costs had dropped four percent between 1975 and 1983, because productivity gains had outpaced labour costs for employers in each year from 1975 to 1983, with the result that for the entire period, productivity had increased by 19 percent, while wage costs had increased by only 14 percent.[49]

The percentage of profits reinvested, on the other hand, had dropped from an average rate of 60 percent in the 1972-75 period, to 30 percent in 1982-83, despite a real increase in profits for the period. The unions argued, then, that increases in profits had not led to increases in investment. Hence the argument that wage restraint would lead to increased profits which in turn would lead to higher investment and increased employment was bogus. What was needed was an active employment program through public investment, and a significant reduction in working time to create more jobs.[50]

The reduction of work time was a central issue of the 1984 collective bargaining round. Some industrial unions pushed for a reduction of working time to 35 hours at the same time as employers were asking for more flexible working schedules in their individual firms to make better use of labour. A compromise settlement was reached only after large scale industrial action in the metalworking and printing industries. The average work week was reduced to 38.5 hours with no loss of pay, and employ-

ers obtained a provision for flexible schedules
above and below this figure provided that the average was attained over a period of two months.   In
addition, the workers in these industries received
an increase of 2.5 to 3 percent for 1984 and 2 percent for 1985.[51]

In other industries, settlements involving
reduced work time were made without recourse to
industrial action.   In the construction, food,
textile, insurance and hotel industries an agreement
for earlier worker retirement was facilitated when
the government committed the employment service to
paying a part of the attendant costs.   The workers
in these industries also received a 3.5 percent
increase, the average settlement for all industries
in 1984.[52]

Slowly, then, the unions were attaining some of
their demands.   Given the demonstration effect of
key settlements in German industrial relations,
similar work reduction provisions will also be
implemented in other industries.   Employer
organisations appear willing to concede these
changes provided that their costs remain reasonable.
Their counter-demands will continue to be for more
diversified pay schemes that will allow them, for
example, to pay lower rates for less experienced
workers and to vary pay rates between more
productive and less productive plants in the same
industry, as well as between relatively declining
and growing sectors in the interest of structural
adjustment and greater international competitiveness.[53]   However, such demands, though supported by
the Council of Economic Experts,[54] will be difficult
for unions to accept because of the tradition of
worker solidarity and because of union politics.

CONCLUSION

Although the Federal Republic of Germany has had an
enviable record of low rates of inflation, attributable in good part to moderate income claims by
German labour, it is not easy to derive practical
lessons from that experience which would be of benefit to other states.   One reason for this has to do
with the difficulty of transferring practices and
institutions from one socioeconomic context to
another, a difficulty that has long been recognised
by social scientists specialising in comparative
politics and comparative public policy.   The difficulty of applying possible German lessons from the

income policy sector in other settings is increased
due to the fact that German income developments have
been little influenced by direct government action
which might be copied elsewhere, but are more a
result of structural and societal features that are,
in many respects, unique to the FRG and, of course,
are not susceptible to transfer elsewhere.

Thus the relative moderation in pay claims by
German labour is a result of Germany's unique situation after World War II with its emphasis on rebuilding; of the consensual nature of German society
brought about by the discrediting of radical left-
and right-wing ideologies and movements; of the relationship between the DGB and the SPD; of the way
in which unions are organised and their approach to
pay bargaining; and of the reliance in the FRG on
the legal system to resolve disputes, a feature of
German society which is demonstrated in the highly
juridicalised industrial relations system.   The
coincidence of these features have much to do with
the high degree of German labour peace and the con-
sequent moderation in worker pay claims.

The constitutional/legal prohibition of governmental interference with 'Tarifautonomie' as interpreted by the courts is also an important factor in
understanding German incomes developments and is
also a feature that is not readily transferable to
other settings, especially since this is a provision
limiting government, and hence one to which few
governments would want to be subjected.   It is one
component, albeit a special one in the sense that it
is legally mandated, of the German approach to
economic policy that is characterised by limited
government interference, an approach that was the
essence of Erhard's 'social market' economy.   This
approach was altered somewhat, as we have seen, in
the late sixties and early seventies when Keynesianism was practised under Schiller, but the perceived failure of 'economic fine-tuning' saw a
return to a greater reliance on market forces and on
Bundesbank monetary policy which have been the main-
stays of government economic policy since that time.

Government involvement with incomes developments has varied in a similar fashion.   In the
period from 1949 to 1966 there was no attempt at
formulating   an   incomes   policy,   given   Erhard's
philosophy and given the prevailing economic conditions.   With greater interventionism came Schiller's
experiments with concerted action, but that experiment foundered practically after a time because of
inaccurate government forecasts of economic develop-

ments, because of the resentment of workers at
having their income lag behind as a result of undue
pay demand restraint based on these forecasts, and
because of very different expectations about concerted action held by government, employers and
unions, the central actors involved in the process.
When the unions finally withdrew from concerted
action in 1977 largely on a pretext, the institution
had long since ceased to have a major impact on
income developments or on economic policy generally.
Thus these tripartite corporatist consultations,
which were sometimes touted by foreign observers as
being instrumental in the relative German success at
dealing with the economic problems of the late sixties and early seventies, were neither enduring nor
of great importance.   In their wake has come a return to the exhortation and moral suasion which were
Erhard's means of affecting developments in key pay
rounds, albeit in more institutionalised settings
which take the form of regular bilateral government-
employer and government-union consultations.

    That the German government's approach to the
income policy sector has been reasonably successful
cannot be denied, given the FRG's low inflation rate
and its economic performance generally, especially
in the decades of the fifties and sixties which were
marked by strong growth, high employment and low
inflation.   Ironically, Germany's series of highest
pay settlements and highest inflation rates came
during the era of concerted action, and it was these
developments which helped to discredit that institution.   Even during this period, however, German
inflation rates were moderate by international
standards and its economic performance compared
favourably to that of other advanced industrialised
countries.   The German experience with even limited
government interference in income developments,
then, has been negative, and hence the return to the
hands-off attitude in the last dozen years.

    Overall, the German approach to income deter-
mination has been comparatively successful in the
difficult economic conditions of the most recent
period.   Inflation has been kept under control by a
combination of a restrictive monetary and conservative fiscal policies.   The employee side has had to
bear much of the burden of the economic difficulties
in terms of low pay increases and a high unemployment rate.   Unions have had little choice but to
accept this burden, given the composition of the
present government, the nature of the industrial
relations system and the society in which it

operates, and the absence of any obvious economic alternatives. Nonetheless, the adjustments in work time provide evidence that employers and government have been willing to accommodate the concerns of the unions. While further adjustments will not be easy, there is no reason to suspect that the German industrial relations system cannot cope with them. One thing appears even more certain: these adjustments will be made without engendering a high level of inflation.

FOOTNOTES

1. Clarence L. Barber and John C.P. McCallum, Controlling Inflation (James Lorimer and Company, Toronto, 1982), p. 54.

2. Richard Medley, 'Inflation Policy in Germany: The Institutional and Political Determinants' in Richard Medley (ed.), The Politics of Inflation (Pergamon Press, London, 1982), p. 132.

3. The following section is based in good part on Volker Berghahn and Detlev Karstens, German Labour Relations (Berg Publishers, Leamington Spa, forthcoming).

4. Arnold J. Heidenheimer and Donald P. Kommers, The Governments of Germany (Thomas Y. Crowell, New York, 1975), p. 132.

5. Eric Owen Smith, 'West Germany' in Eric Owen Smith (ed.), Trade Unions in the Developed Economies, (Croom Helm, London, 1981), pp. 180-81.

6. C.C. Schweitzer et al., Politics and Government in the Federal Republic of Germany, Basic Documents (Berg Publishers Limited, Leamington Spa, 1984), p.232.

7. Smith, 'West Germany', p. 189.

8. Industrial Democracy in Europe, European Industrial Relations (Clarendon Press, Oxford, 1981), p. 82.

9. A comprehensive critique of codetermination from the employee perspective is presented in Wilhelm Adamy and Johannes Steffen, Handbuch der Arbeitsbeziehungen (Bundescentrale fuer politische Bildung, Bonn, 1985), pp. 185-214.

10. Smith, 'West Germany', p. 196.

11. Berghahn and Karstens, forthcoming.

12. Organization for Economic Co-operation and Development, Collective Bargaining and Government Policies in Ten OECD Countries (Paris, 1979), p. 58.

13. Berghahn and Karstens, forthcoming.

14. Joachim Bergmann et al., Gewerkschaften in der Bundesrepublik Vol. 1 (Campus Verlag, Frankfurt/

New York, 1979), p. 81.
15.   Calculated from data in Norbert Kloten, Karl-Heinz Ketterer and Rainer Vollmer, 'West Germany's Stabilization Performance' in Leon N. Lindberg and Charles S. Maier (eds.), The Politics of Inflation and Economic Stagnation (The Brookings Institution, Washington, 1985), p. 355.
16.   Andrei S. Markovits and Christopher Allen 'Trade Unions and the Economic Crisis: The West German Case' in Peter Gourevitch et al., Unions and Economic Crisis: Britain, West Germany and Sweden (George Allen and Unwin, London, 1984), p. 122.
17.   Ibid., p. 123.
18.   Ibid., p. 125.
19.   Ibid., p. 126.
20.   Kloten et al., 'West Germany's Stabilization', p. 370.
21.   Medley, 'Inflation Policy', p. 133.
22.   Kloten et al., 'West Germany's Stabilization', p. 372.
23.   Bergman et al, Gewerkschaften, pp. 91-94.
24.   The following discussion relies in part on Peter Weber, 'Die Konzertierte Aktion und andere Versuche der Einbindung der Tarifpartner in das Gesamtinteresse,' (Seminar fuer Wirtschaftswissenschaft und Didaktik der Wirtschaftslehre, University of Bonn, 1985, unpublished paper). See also Hermann Adam, Die Konzertierte Aktion in der Bundesrepublik (Cologne, Bund-Verlag, 1972) and Michael Zink, Konzertierte Aktion und Gewerkschaftspolitik in der Bundesrepublik Deutschland (Munich, 1975).
25.   Kloten et al., 'West Germany's Stabilization', p. 376.
26.   Robert J. Flanagan, David W. Soskice and Lloyd Ulman, Unionism, Economic Stabilization and Incomes Policy (The Brookings Institution, Washington, 1983), p. 281.
27.   Kloten et al., 'West Germany's Stabilization', p. 377.
28.   Markovits and Allen, 'Trade Unions', p. 135.
29.   Kloten et al., 'West Germany's Stabilization', p. 358.
30.   Markovits and Allen, 'Trade Unions', p.
31.   Kloten et al., 'West Germany's Stabilization', p. 389.
32.   Ibid., p. 358.
33.   Markovits and Allen, 'Trade Unions', p. 148.
34.   Kloten et al., 'West Germany's Stabilization', p. 358.

35. Markovits and Allen, 'Trade Unions', p. 144.
36. Ibid., p. 150.
37. Kloten et al., 'West Germany's Stabilization', pp. 355, 358.
38. Deutscher Gewerkschaftsbund, 1981, Grundsatz-Programm des Deutschen Gewerkschaftsbundes (Duesseldorf, 1981), pp. 11-12.
39. Ibid., pp. 14-21.
40. Ibid., p. 12 and Markovits and Allen 'Trade Unions', p. 158.
41. Deutscher Gewerkschaftsbund, 'Grundsatz-Programm', p. 8.
42. Interview by author with DGB official, Duesseldorf, December, 1985.
43. Kloten et al., 'West Germany's Stabilization', p. 355.
44. Council of Economic Experts, 1981-82 Annual Report, p. 174.
45. Ibid.
46. Council of Economic Experts, 1982-83 Annual Report, p. 67.
47. Council of Economic Experts, 1983-84 Annual Report, pp. 84-88.
48. Deutscher Gewerkschaftsbund, Wirtschafts-politische Informationen No. 1, 1984 (Duesseldorf, 1984), pp. 4-5.
49. Ibid., p. 7.
50. Ibid., pp. 4-5, 10-11.
51. Council of Economic Experts, 1984-85 Annual Report, pp. 78-79.
52. Ibid.
53. Interview by author with BDA official, Cologne, December, 1985.
54. Council of Economic Experts, 1982-83 Annual Report, p. 141.

REFERENCES

Adam, Hermann, Die Konzertierte Aktion in der Bundesrepublik (Cologne, Bund-Verlag, 1972)
Adamy, Wilhelm and Steffen, Johannes, Handbuch der Arbeitsbeziehungen (Bundescentrale fuer politische Bildung, Bonn, 1985)
Barber, Clarence L. and McCallum, John C.P., Controlling Inflation (James Lorimer and Company, Toronto, 1982)
Berghahn, Volker and Karstens, Detlev, German Labour Relations (Berg Publishers, Leamington Spa, forthcoming)

Bergmann, Joachim, Jacobi, Otto and Mueller-Jentsch,
    Walter, Gewerkschaften in der Bundesrepublik,
    Vol. 1 (Campus Verlag, Frankfurt/New York,
    1979)
Deutscher Bundestag, Council of Economic Experts
    1981-82 Annual Report (Bonn, 1982)
Deutscher Bundestag, Council of Economic Experts
    1982-83 Annual Report (Bonn, 1983)
Deutscher Bundestag, Council of Economic Experts
    1983-84 Annual Report (Bonn, 1984)
Deutscher Bundestag, Council of Economic Experts
    1984-85 Annual Report (Bonn, 1985)
Deutscher Gewerkschaftsbund, 1981 Grundsatz-
    Programm des Deutschen Gewerkschaftsbundes
    (Duesseldorf, 1981)
Deutscher Gewerkschaftsbund, Wirtschaftspolitische
    Informationen, No. 1 (Duesseldorf, 1984)
Flanagan, Robert J., Soskice, David W. and Ulman,
    Lloyd, Unionism, Econimic Stabilization and
    Incomes Policy (The Brookings Institution,
    Washington, 1983)
Heidenheimer, Arnold J. and Kommers, Donald P., The
    Governments of Germany (Thomas Y. Crowell, New
    York, 1975)
Kloten, Norbert, Ketterer, Karl-Heinz and Vollmer,
    Rainer, 'West Germany's Stabilization Perfor-
    mance', in Lindberg, Leon N. and Maier, Charles
    S. (eds.), The Politics of Inflation and
    Economic Stagnation (The Brookings Institution,
    Washington, 1985)
Markovits, Andrei S. and Allen, Christopher, 'Trade
    Unions and the Economic Crisis: The West
    German Case', in Gourevitch, Peter et al.,
    Unions and Economic Crisis: Britain, West
    Germany and Sweden (George Allen and Unwin,
    London, 1984)
Medley, Richard, 'Inflation Policy in Germany: The
    Institutional and Political Determinants', in
    Medley, Richard (ed.), The Politics of Infla-
    tion (Pergamon Press, London, 1982)
Organization for Economic Co-operation and Develop-
    ment, Collective Bargaining and Government
    Policies in Ten OECD Countries (Paris, 1979)
Smith, Eric Owen, 'West Germany', in Smith, Eric
    Owen (ed.), Trade Unions in the Developed
    Economies (Croom Helm, London, 1981)
Weber, Peter, 'Die Konzertierte Aktion und andere
    Versuche der Einbindung der Tarifpartner in das
    Gesamtinteresse' (Seminar fuer Wirtschaftswis-
    senschaft und Didaktik der Wirtschaftslehre,
    University of Bonn, 1985, unpublished paper).

Germany: Life Without an Incomes Policy

Zink, Michael, Konzertierte Aktion und Gewerk
    schaftspolitik in der Bundesrepublik Deutsch
    land (Munich, 1975)

178

ABBREVIATIONS

ACPI	Advisory Committee on Prices and Incomes (Australia)
BNA Act	British North America Act
AFL-CIO	American Federation of Labour - Congress of Industrial Organisations
AIA	Anti-Inflation Administrator (Canada)
AIB	Anti-Inflation Board (Canada)
ACTU	Australian Council of Trade Unions
BDA	Bund Deutcher Arbeitsgeber
	Bund Deutscher Industrien
CAI	Confederation of Australian Industry
CCAA	Commonwealth Conciliation and Arbitration Act
CCPS	Cabinet Committee on Price Stability (U.S.)
CEA	Council of Economic Advisers (U.S.)
CIM	Commission on Industry and Manpower (Britain)
CISC	Construction Industry Stabilisation Committee (U.S.)
CLC	Canadian Labour Congress
CLC	Cost of Living Council (U.S.)
COLA	Cost of living allowance
CPI	Consumer Price Index
CSIP	Centre for the Study of Inflation and Productivity (Canada)
	Deutsche Angestellen Gewerkschaft
DBB	Deutsche Bundesbank
DEA	Department of Economic Affairs (Britain)
DGB	Deutscher Gewerkschaftsbund
DIHT	Deutscher Industrie und Handelstag
EEC	European Economic Community
EPAC	Economic Planning Advisory Council (Australia)
FRG	Federal Republic of Germany
GDP	Gross domestic product
GDR	German Democratic Republic
GNP	Gross national product
IAC	Industries Assistance Commission (Australia)
ILO	International Labour Organisation
NBPI	National Board for Prices and Incomes (Britain)
NECD	National Economic Development Council (Britain)
NIC	National Incomes Commission (Britain)
OECD	Organisation for Economic Co-operation and Development
OPA	Office of Price Administration (U.S.)
OPEC	Organisation of Petroleum Exporting

179

	Countries
PIC	Prices and Incomes Commission (Canada)
PJT	Prices Justification Tribunal (Australia)
PSA	Prices Surveillance Authority (Australia)
TUC	Trades Union Congress (Britain)
UAW	United Automobile Workers
USWA	United Steelworkers of America
WIB	War Industries Board (U.S.)
WSB	Wage Stabilisation Board (U.S.)

CONTRIBUTORS

Beth Bilson is Assistant Vice-President (Administration) and Associate Professor of
law, University of Saskatchewan,
Canada.

Jown Lawler is Associate Professor of Industrial
Relations, Institute of Labor and
Industrial Relations, University of
Illinois at Urbana-Champaign.

Hans J. Michelmann is Professor of Political
Studies, University of Saskatchewan,
Canada.

Malcolm Rimmer is Senior Lecturer in Industrial
Relations, Australian Graduate School
of Management in the University of New
South Wales, Australia.

INDEX

185

Constitution 4, 152, 172
Constitutional Court 150, 165
Council of Economic Experts 157, 158, 159, 160, 161, 169, 170, 171
Deutsche Angestellen Gewerkschaft 147, 161
Deutsche Bundesbank 153, 154, 156, 158, 161, 167, 172
Deutscher Beamtenbund 147, 161
Deutscher Gewerkschaftsbund 146, 147, 160, 163, 165, 172
Deutscher Industrie und Handelstag 148, 161
economic framework plan 168
exports 146
German Chamber of Industry and Commerce 148
German Christian Trade Union Movement 147
German Trade Union Federation 146
Grand Coalition 146, 147, 158
industrial relations 144, 146, 159, 171
labour courts 151
Laender 151, 152, 156
liberal party 145
Meinhold formula 155
Social Democratic party 145, 155, 162, 167, 172
social market economy 146, 172
Stability and Growth Act 158
Tarifautonomie 150, 159, 162, 172
Third Reich 145
Volkswagenwerk 152

Weimer Republic 145
Work Promotion Act 166
works councils 148
Federal-provincial agreements 123
Flanders, Allan 63
Fraser, Malcolm 101, 107, 115
Friderichs, Hans 164
Friedman, Milton 20
Full employment 14, 48, 59

German Chamber of Industry and Commerce 148
see also Deutscher Industrie und Handelstag
German Christian Trade Union Movement 147
German Democratic Republic 145, 153
German Trade Union Federation 146
see also Deutscher Gewerkschaftsbund
Great Britain
blacklist 58
Commission for Industry and Manpower 55
Confederation of British Industry 54
Conservative party 46, 47, 50, 51, 55, 59
Council on Productivity, Prices and Incomes 49
Department of Economic Affairs 52
guiding light 50
Industrial Relations Act 57
Labour party 46, 47, 48, 49, 50, 55
n-1, 56
National Board for Prices and Incomes 51, 52, 54, 62, 63, 66, 69

For Product Safety Concerns and Information please contact our
EU representative GPSR@taylorandfrancis.com Taylor & Francis
Verlag GmbH, Kaufingerstraße 24, 80331 München, Germany